OXFORD WORLD'S CLASSICS

LAOZI

Daodejing

Translated with Notes by
EDMUND RYDEN

With an Introduction by
BENJAMIN PENNY

OXFORD
UNIVERSITY PRESS

OXFORD

UNIVERSITY PRESS

Great Clarendon Street, Oxford OX2 6DP

Oxford University Press is a department of the University of Oxford.
It furthers the University's objective of excellence in research, scholarship,
and education by publishing worldwide in

Oxford New York

Auckland Cape Town Dar es Salaam Hong Kong Karachi
Kuala Lumpur Madrid Melbourne Mexico City Nairobi
New Delhi Shanghai Taipei Toronto

With offices in

Argentina Austria Brazil Chile Czech Republic France Greece
Guatemala Hungary Italy Japan Poland Portugal Singapore
South Korea Switzerland Thailand Turkey Ukraine Vietnam

Oxford is a registered trade mark of Oxford University Press
in the UK and in certain other countries

Published in the United States
by Oxford University Press Inc., New York

Translation, commentary, notes, and other editorial matter © Edmund Ryden 2008
Introduction © Benjamin Penny 2008

The moral rights of the authors have been asserted
Database right Oxford University Press (maker)

First published as an Oxford World's Classics paperback 2008

British Library Cataloguing in Publication Data

Data available

Library of Congress Cataloging-in-Publication Data

Laozi.
[Dao de jing. English]
Daodejing / Laozi; translated with notes by Edmund Ryden; with an introduction
by Benjamin Penny.
p. cm.—(Oxford world's classics)
Includes bibliographical references (p.).
ISBN 978-0-19-920855-5
I. Ryden, Edmund. II. Title.
BL1900.L26E5 2008b
299.5′1482—dc22

2008011595

Typeset by Cepha Imaging Private Ltd., Bangalore, India
Printed and bound in Great Britain by Clays Ltd, Elcograf S.p.A.

ISBN 978-0-19-920855-5

OXFORD WORLD'S CLASSICS

DAODEJING

The *Daodejing* or *Classic of the Way and the Life Force* dates from the fifth to fourth centuries BCE and is the best-loved of all classical Chinese texts. The author or editor is thought to have been someone who rejected the scholastic philosophy of Master Kong (Confucius) in favour of a way of thinking that was closer to nature. Deliberately void of all proper names—even the author is known only as the Old Master (Laozi)—the text is set in an eternal and universal present. Revered as a religious classic by Chinese Daoists, it is not only one of the foundational texts of Chinese thought, but has been rightly acknowledged as one of the most inspiring books in world literature.

EDMUND RYDEN teaches at Fujen University in Taiwan. He was the first director of the John Paul II Peace Institute at Fujen University and has edited a series of conference papers in the field of human rights. Among his other publications is a translation of Zhang Dai-nian's *Key Concepts of Chinese Philosophy* (2002).

BENJAMIN PENNY is Fellow in the History of China in the Research School of Pacific and Asian Studies at the Australian National University. He is the editor of *Biography and Religion in China and Tibet* (2002) and *Daoism in History: Essays in Honour of Liu Ts'un-yan* (2006).

OXFORD WORLD'S CLASSICS

*For over 100 years Oxford World's Classics have brought
readers closer to the world's great literature. Now with over 700
titles—from the 4,000-year-old myths of Mesopotamia to the
twentieth century's greatest novels—the series makes available
lesser-known as well as celebrated writing.*

*The pocket-sized hardbacks of the early years contained
introductions by Virginia Woolf, T. S. Eliot, Graham Greene,
and other literary figures which enriched the experience of reading.
Today the series is recognized for its fine scholarship and
reliability in texts that span world literature, drama and poetry,
religion, philosophy and politics. Each edition includes perceptive
commentary and essential background information to meet the
changing needs of readers.*

CONTENTS

INTRODUCTION

> How easily we can find our own image in the *Daodejing*! It
> is a magic mirror, always found to reflect our concept of
> the truth.[1]

The *Daodejing* is one of the foundational texts of Chinese
thought. Its fortunes have risen and fallen with different dynasties and regimes, with influential scholars and writers acclaiming
it as a pre-eminent work of the Chinese tradition or damning it as
metaphysical nonsense. Nonetheless, it has been a feature on the
landscape of learned Chinese people for more than two millennia.
In more recent times the *Daodejing* has become known and been
celebrated beyond the Chinese world. First translated into
French in 1841, and into English in 1868, it has been re-translated
numerous times, with ever more versions appearing today in elec-
tronic form. Some of these versions are serious attempts at
making sense of a famously difficult text, but many more have
little to do with the original; as little, perhaps, as that stream of
books whose titles begin with 'The Tao of...'.

As interest in the *Daodejing* has become more widespread
and as its popularity as a text for translation has grown, it has
sometimes been considered as a philosophical gem suspended in
a historical and cultural void, removed from its ancient Chinese
context. Without this context, some translators and writers on
the *Daodejing* have dressed it in clothes of their own choosing,
often inappropriately. Strangely, this process has taken place at
the same time as our knowledge of the origins of the text has increased immeasurably. In the west, as Sinology developed in the
nineteenth and twentieth centuries, and as our familiarity with
the wealth of literature from ancient China grew, so our knowledge of the conceptual world of that time and place broadened
and became more nuanced. Indeed, from the 1970s remarkable

---

[1] Holmes Welch, *The Parting of the Way: Lao-tzu and the Taoist Movement* (London:
Methuen and Co., 1957), 13.

archaeological discoveries—particularly the texts on silk and bamboo strips unearthed from Mawangdui near Changsha in Hunan in 1972–4 and Guodian near Jingmen in Hubei in 1993—have caused our ideas about the origins and composition of the *Daodejing* to be revised in fundamental ways. We are, therefore, in the extraordinary position of being more informed about the original *Daodejing* now than any reader for the last 1,500 years or more. This new translation takes these discoveries into full account, restoring the context in which the *Daodejing* came into being.

Reading the Daodejing

The *Daodejing* is traditionally ascribed to Laozi, a title that simply means 'the old master'. Who this 'old master' was, or if there really was such a person, has been a subject of discussion since at least the first century before the Common Era. Similarly, when he lived—and therefore when the *Daodejing* was written—has long been a matter of dispute. The version of the *Daodejing* that has been handed down to us—known as the 'Wang Bi edition'—probably derives from the third century CE, although it is clear that versions of the text much like it were circulating some 500 years earlier. The Wang Bi edition is also the text most familiar to western readers as, until the 1980s, it formed the basis for all the translations into European languages. It has eighty-one short chapters divided into two sections. The first section consists of thirty-seven chapters and goes under the name of the *Daojing*, since its opening chapter focuses on the *Dao*, or Way. The second section has forty-four chapters and is known as the *Dejing*, as Chapter 38, the first in this section, concentrates on the *De*—Life Force or Vitality. Thus the *Daojing* and the *Dejing* together form the *Daodejing*, the name by which the text is often known today.

One reason why the *Daodejing* has generated so many studies and translations is that the text itself can be read in a multiplicity of ways, both in a strictly grammatical sense, and in terms of its content. Chinese texts from before the twentieth century are written in a language that is usually called literary Chinese. Terse and economical in expression, literary Chinese can be technically precise as well as capable of great beauty, happily rendering both dry bureaucratic instructions and delicately evocative poetry and prose. Some writers, in fact, composed fine examples of official documents in their role as government functionaries while also exchanging verse with their friends. Literary Chinese is notable, however, for its lack of punctuation: it has no commas and full stops, no paragraph markings, no fixed parts of speech, and, of course, no capital letters. Deciding where one sentence ends and the next begins, for instance, might seem like a challenge (and it sometimes is), but usually texts in literary Chinese are clear, as particular characters often act as grammatical markers, doing the work of punctuation and spacing in western texts. One of the problems with the Wang Bi edition, discussed at greater length below, is that its use of such particles, as these characters are called, is rather limited. In other words, a reader does not have the benefit of many of the grammatical markers we might expect, and do indeed find, in other ancient Chinese texts. Even for skilled Chinese readers of literary Chinese, therefore, there are important points of genuine ambiguity in the *Daodejing*, where two or more readings of certain passages are equally possible.

In addition to these grammatical considerations, the *Daodejing* also has a particular mode of expression: aphoristic, sometimes enigmatic, and often counter-intuitive. The Way, as readers will note almost as soon as they encounter the text, is not easily characterized. We encounter this difficulty in the opening chapter of the book, where the Way is described in terms of what it is not, rather than what it is:

> Of ways you may speak,
>   but not the Perennial Way;
> By names you may name,
>   but not the Perennial Name.

Here, the Way is represented in its most general aspect as, perhaps, befits the opening lines of the text—although, as we will see, the position that these lines occupied in the *Daodejing* may not always have been the same. One of the reasons why the Way is described in negative terms is that it cannot be adequately defined by making positive statements about it, even knowing what to call it. The *Daodejing* addresses this issue explicitly in. Chapter 25:

> I do not know her name; I entitle her the Way;
> I force myself to name her Great.

For the same reasons, the Way is also sometimes defined paradoxically, thus:

> Looking at her, you will not see her;
> Listening to her, you will not hear her,
> Yet she cannot be used up.
>
> (Ch. 35)

However, the most pervasive manner in which the Way is characterized in the *Daodejing* is by using metaphor—the Way is like a gully, a mother, the course of a river, or a path or road. In fact, the word *dao* is not exclusive to the *Daodejing* but is used by many Chinese philosophical texts to describe their teachings. A 'Way' is put into practice by walking a particular road, and someone who does this is, therefore, a 'Way-farer' in this translation. However, readers expecting to find easy or direct insight into how to become such a Way-farer, according to the *Daodejing*—in contrast with other, more straightforward, philosophical texts of ancient China—may struggle to find instruction: these Way-farers are 'unseen, mysterious, communing with the abstruse, deep so they could not be fathomed' (Ch. 15).

Thus, to define the nature of the Way, it is necessary to place these metaphors in the foreground, to begin with the images used in the *Daodejing* to clarify how the Way is characterized.[2] Metaphor, here, is understood to be much more than a literary decoration; it is a way of writing that reveals meaningful relationships between objects and processes and is crucial to an understanding of the text. However, before discussing the use of metaphor in the

---

[2] This approach follows that of Sarah Allan, especially as demonstrated in her book *The Way of Water and the Sprouts of Virtue* (Albany: SUNY Press, 1997).

Daodejing in detail, it is important to give some background into one specific aspect of ancient Chinese thought.

In ancient China, the workings of the cosmos were often understood in terms of 'correlative cosmology' by authors across a range of philosophical schools. This was a way of thinking in which features of the natural world and the changes that transformed them were grouped in sets—notably of two, where the core structuring pair was *yin* and *yang*, but also of five in the form of the elemental phases of wood, earth, fire, water, and metal, and sixty-four in the hexagrams of the *Yijing*, or *Book of Changes*. Countless aspects of the world formed pairs in parallel to the *yang* and *yin*—heaven/earth, male/female, ruler/minister, summer/winter, stretching/contracting, above/below, father/son, and so on. Thus, heaven, male, and ruler were correlated with *yang*, and earth, female, and minister were correlated with *yin*. It is important to remember that these pairs refer to complementary relationships rather than to intrinsic features: in ancient China, a minister (*yin*), for instance, would certainly have been male (*yang*), and be both a father (*yang*) and a son (*yin*).[3]

The terms *yin* and *yang* appear only once in the *Daodejing* (in Chapter 42), but the use of complementary pairs that pervades *yin-yang* thinking is a recurrent feature in the text. Furthermore, the Way is consistently compared with characteristics that are correlated with *yin*. It is 'the mother of the myriad things' (Ch. 1) and 'the mother of the world' (Chs. 25, 52), 'the gully's spirit' and 'the mysterious cleft' (Ch. 6), it is like water that floods (Chs. 8, 34), it is characterized by reversal and weakness (Ch. 40). One of the most notable features of this translation is that it takes these characterizations seriously, by rendering the Way as female. In literary Chinese gender is not marked, so the translator must decide on the most appropriate English word to use when a pronoun is required: in this translation the pronoun chosen for the Way is 'she'. It should be emphasized that this femaleness of the

---

[3] On correlative cosmology, see A. C. Graham, *Yin-Yang and the Nature of Correlative Thinking* (Singapore: Institute of East Asian Philosophies, 1986).

Way is derived from the images used to describe it rather than female gender being marked in the language of the text.

A similar pattern of imagery is used to describe the figure of the Sage in the *Daodejing*. Generally taken to be the person who epitomizes the teachings of a particular school of philosophy, how he should behave depends, of course, on the nature of the teachings concerned. Indeed, in one of the few references in the *Daodejing* to other philosophical schools of ancient China, it says that the figure of the Sage is 'not benevolent' (Ch. 5), a statement in direct opposition to Confucian teachings where benevolence is a key virtue. Since the Sage is the one who embodies the Way, he takes on her typically *yin* characteristics. He 'holds himself back' (Ch. 7); he is like 'a baby that has not yet smiled' who appreciates sucking milk from its mother, who as we have seen is the Way herself (Ch. 20); he does not compete but, rather, bends (Ch. 22); he does not act and does not grasp (Ch. 64); he is compared to the hen, the 'valley of the world', and reverts to the state of an infant (Ch. 28). In fact, it is in the Sage's not acting that one of the most characteristic ideas of the *Daodejing* is revealed, namely, that precisely by not acting, everything can be accomplished:

> A person given to the Way makes daily regress.
> Regress and again regress, until coming to not acting.
> When not acting then there is nothing not done.
>
> (Ch. 48)

Like the Sage, the state that embodies the Way acts by not acting. This might appear counter-intuitive, especially in the China of the period when the *Daodejing* was composed, aptly described in Chinese history as the 'Warring States'. During the roughly two centuries prior to the unification of China under the Qin dynasty in 221 BCE, seven quasi-independent states fought to conquer each other in a drive for supremacy. It comes as no surprise, therefore, that this is the period in which the classic text of military strategy, Sunzi's *Art of War*, was written. What must have appeared surprising for a contemporary reader, however, was how the *Daodejing* recommended that a great state behave:

> A great state is like a river's lower course,
> She is the feminine aspect of the world.

In the mating of the world:
The feminine always conquers the masculine by stillness.
It is because of her stillness that she is apt to take the lower position.

(Ch. 61)

The great state follows the lowest course as water flows downward, it is still rather than active, and adopts the feminine as its model—yet this is precisely how it conquers.

Some passages such as these in the *Daodejing* that concern political entities have given rise to the idea that it is essentially a book about statecraft and government. This is hinted at in other sections where advice is given to a ruler, or to a ruler's counsellors:

One who helps the lord of men according to the Way,
Does not use arms to subdue the world since such actions easily rebound.

(Ch. 30)

Or:

Of old, those who fared by the Way
Did not use her to enlighten the people, rather to fool them.

Difficulty in governing people comes from their knowing too much.

(Ch. 65)

Another perspective sees the *Daodejing* as primarily interested in self-cultivation. Traditions of 'nourishing life', as it was known in ancient times, have existed since records began in China. These methods involved physical or mental meditations, special diets or sexual practices, and prescriptions for both moral behaviour and for medicines. Those who pursued such activities were aiming to lengthen their lives, ideally to the ultimate condition of immortality. At the time the *Daodejing* was composed adepts practised various methods of self-cultivation, and there are passages in the text where we can see references to breathing exercises involving particular forms of inhalation and exhalation, such as in the use of the metaphor of the bellows and the blow-tube in Chapter 5.

However, if the *Daodejing* was originally intended as a manual for self-cultivation, it could not serve that purpose today. In fact, even when it was composed it is hard to imagine how its enigmatic aphorisms could have been used to convey specific instructions.

It may be best to think of the *Daodejing*—or parts of it—as a kind of pedagogical tool or mnemonic device that would have been used as a starting-point in discussion or practice between a master and a pupil. If some of the sayings of the *Daodejing* were used as prompts for more extensive explanations in the context of teaching, we have lost the elaborations that a teacher might have used in their instruction.

The Text of the Daodejing

Another layer of complexity is added to how we view the *Daodejing* and its interpretation when we consider fundamental questions related to the actual text itself.[4] It is to be expected that books from ancient times will have suffered as they were passed down from generation to generation. Especially in the days before printing and mass publication, mistakes were made in copying, parts of books could be destroyed by fire or flood or mould, books would pass out of favour for a period and be lost or forgotten, the comments of commentators could be absorbed into the main text, misguided editors could excise passages they thought were late additions or change some words they did not understand. The *Daodejing* was no more immune from these tribulations than any other ancient book. In addition, though, aspects of the early history of the *Daodejing* that have been revealed to us through archaeology have complicated our understanding of the nature of the original text.

For many centuries, until modern times, the picture was relatively simple. The *Daodejing* came down to us in various editions to which were typically attached commentaries of various kinds. As noted above, the most commonly accepted version of the *Daodejing* (also known as the 'classical' or received version) is associated with the name of Wang Bi (226–49 CE), a scholar who lived under the State of Wei during the period of the Three Kingdoms.

---

[4] For a brief overview of textual matters related to the *Daodejing*, see William G. Boltz, 'Lao tzu Tao te ching', in Michael Loewe (ed.), *Early Chinese Texts: A Bibliographical Guide* (Berkeley: Society for the Study of Early China and the Institute of East Asian Studies, University of California, 1993), 269–92.

Wang is best known for his commentaries to the *Daodejing* and the *Yijing*, or *Book of Changes*. The version of the *Daodejing* that goes under his name may not, in fact, have been exactly the version he used, and this edition itself probably belongs to a textual tradition associated with the other major early commentary, that goes under the name of Heshanggong (the 'master who lives by the river'). The date of the Heshanggong commentary, and therefore the text it is attached to, is also uncertain, but clearly this line of texts goes back to early medieval times, not long after the fall of the Han dynasty in the early third century. There are minor differences in the texts associated with the Wang Bi and Heshanggong commentaries (and some others in this line of transmission), but none of them affects the meaning of any passages.

The first major challenge to this way of viewing the text of the *Daodejing* came in the early 1970s, when three tombs were opened at a site at Mawangdui in the suburbs of the city of Changsha in southern China.[5] These three tombs belonged to Li Cang, marquis of Dai, who died in 186 BCE, his wife, known as Lady Dai, who died after 168 BCE, and a second man, in all probability their son, who predeceased his mother in 168 BCE. The tombs contained an extraordinary collection of artefacts, including two magnificent painted silk banners, lacquerware, musical instruments, and much else. The tomb of the son also contained the texts of books written on silk; some of these were extant, some were of books whose titles were known from ancient bibliographies but had been lost, and some were previously unknown. Two of the texts were versions of the *Daodejing* that have become known as Mawangdui A and Mawangdui B. Since they were found in the tomb of the son of the marquis, we know that both were inscribed before 168 BCE. However, by examining the style in which the characters were written, and observing which particular characters in the text were replaced by others of similar meaning or shape—characters were tabooed if they occurred in the personal names of

---

[5] On the Mawangdui texts, see Robert G. Henricks, *Lao-tzu Te-Tao Ching: A New Translation Based on the Recently Discovered Ma-wang-tui Texts* (New York: Ballantine Books, 1989).

emperors—we can be more specific and say that the 'A' text probably dates from about 200 BCE, and the 'B' text from about twenty years later.

The Mawangdui texts are intriguing for a number of reasons. First, while the Wang Bi edition divides the *Daodejing* into eighty-one chapters, the Mawangdui 'A' text—where new chapters often look to be marked with black dots—appears to have some chapter divisions where the Wang Bi edition has none, and has no division where the Wang Bi edition marks them. In a book where so much of the text is comprised of short aphorisms, context is particularly important; thus, the grouping of passages into chapters can be an important influence on how certain sections of the book are read. Secondly, while the Mawangdui texts divide the eighty-one chapters of the *Daodejing* into two sections like the Wang Bi edition, both of them reverse the order of the two parts. That is, the Mawangdui texts begin with what we have come to know as Chapter 38, and the famous opening chapter of the Wang Bi edition ('Of ways you may speak/but not the Perennial Way, etc.') comes at the beginning of the second section. Thus, since it was the order of the two sections of the book that gave it the traditional title of *Daodejing*, perhaps the Mawangdui texts should reverse the order of the two terms and be known as the *Dedaojing*, or the *Laozi Dedaojing*, as one translator has entitled his book.[6] The third major difference between the Wang Bi family of editions and the Mawangdui texts relates to the classic observation (made in this Introduction as elsewhere) that the *Daodejing* is notoriously ambiguous. One of the greatest differences between the Mawangdui texts and the Wang Bi edition is that they often include the grammatical particles that the latter edition lacks. By doing so, the Mawangdui texts have clarified many of the grammatical conundrums long considered to be characteristic of the *Daodejing*. It has also meant that some of the age-old arguments over which of two possible readings of some passages in the text was correct have now been settled. Not all the puzzles have been solved, but readers of the text are now in a much better position

[6] Ibid.

to know whether what seemed like intentional ambiguity was actually caused simply by the vicissitudes of transmission.

As the scholarly community digested the importance of the Mawangdui texts, argued over their relevance, and recast their views of the original *Daodejing*, in 1993 another excavation a few hundred kilometres north of Mawangdui produced another, even earlier, version of the book.[7] This excavation was at Guodian, near the modern city of Jingmen, a little to the north of the Yangtse River, from a group of tombs close to the ancient capital of the state of Chu. Chu ruled the southern part of China during the period before China was unified by the state of Qin. The tomb from which this *Daodejing* came was sealed between the mid-fourth and early third centuries BCE, and is, thus, possibly 150 years earlier than the tomb at Mawangdui which held the *Daodejing* texts. It probably belonged to the teacher of a royal prince. Rather than being inscribed on silk, these texts were written on the much more common material of bamboo strips. Ancient Chinese books written in this manner were made from many of these strips tied together with string and rolled up—the standard Chinese word for a book chapter actually means 'to roll up'. Over time, the string in these rolls would rot and the strips would be detached from each other. When caches of such strips are found in tombs, they are commonly mixed up in a heap. The first task is, therefore, to work out how they should be reassembled. As at Mawangdui, the *Daodejing* was not the only text found in this cache, which also included other known and unknown writings. Of the 800 strips found at Guodian, some 721 had writing on them, and of these about seventy-one had material associated with the *Daodejing*.

When the strips had been reassembled, the text of this *Daodejing* was different from any extant version.[8] Since the strips

---

[7] On the Guodian finds, see Sarah Allan and Crispin Williams (eds.), *The Guodian Laozi: Proceedings of the International Conference, Dartmouth College, May 1998* (Berkeley: The Society for the Study of Early China and the Institute of East Asian Studies, University of California, 2000).

[8] The following discussion is based on Harold D. Roth, 'Some Methodological Issues in the Study of the Guodian *Laozi* Parallels', in ibid. 71–88.

themselves are of various sizes, and there are marks on them from where the string had bound them together, it appears that the Guodian material was originally in three separate bundles. Comparing the Guodian text with that of the Wang Bi and Mawangdui versions, there is material in the strips from thirty-one of the eighty-one chapters as they appear in later editions. However, the order in which they are found does not correspond with any other version of the text. Only sixteen of these chapters appear 'complete', with some lacking major parts of what we are familiar with from other editions. In total, the Guodian text has only about 40 per cent of the material of the Wang Bi edition. Importantly, if we compare the three bundles, only one section that corresponds to nine lines of the Wang Bi edition is duplicated (in bundles 'A' and 'C').

What, then, is the Guodian material? Is it three parts of the same text or three different texts? Is it—or are they—versions of the *Daodejing*? Or should they be seen as artefacts of textual streams that led, after the intervention of an editor or editors, to the book we know today? If we were to reject the idea that the three bundles make up one complete text, should each of the bundles even be seen as representing something 'whole'?

One possibility is that the three bundles together constitute a selection of passages from an already extant *Daodejing*; in other words, the *Daodejing* as it came to be known later already existed in something like the form we know it in today, and somebody selected the parts they found valuable from it to produce the Guodian material. Arguing against this position is evidence from the lines that are duplicated in bundles 'A' and 'C'. In the nine lines concerned—from what we have come to know as Chapter 64—there are no fewer than thirty-three variations in the texts, including whole lines being transposed. This would indicate strongly that the two versions of this passage could not have been copied from the same source text.

This leaves two other possibilities. The first is that the Guodian material formed one of the sources for the text that eventually became the *Daodejing* as we know it—bearing in mind that we do not know how many or what other sources there might have been. The second is that the sources that led to the *Daodejing* that resembles the Mawangdui or Wang Bi versions also led, in some way, to the Guodian material. If this were true, then the Guodian material and the other extant versions of the *Daodejing* do not exist in any direct ancestral relationship with each other. Without more evidence, it is impossible to decide whether either of these possibilities is likely, but in the light of this discussion we should also bear in mind another consideration. In what we might think of as the 'early days' of the *Daodejing*, passages may not, in fact, have been written down. There is evidence in the various texts that have survived not only of the kind of aphoristic style that might lend itself to memorization, but also of rhyme. That is, the '*Daodejing*'—or the early constituent parts or it, or parts of variants of it—might best be understood as originally existing in oral form, passed between master and student without ever being written down. If this were the case, there almost certainly would have been different sets of passages recited and committed to memory in different contexts; and when it came to writing these passages down, different sets of passages (or selections of passages) would be inscribed on to strips in different sequences by different hands.

Possibly, then, one useful way of seeing the Guodian material is not as a single, unified version of the *Daodejing* but rather as several selections of sayings that may have existed independently from each other, and which came from the circles around different teachers from related schools. Thus, when it comes to relating this material to later versions of the *Daodejing*, comparison is probably best made on a passage-by-passage basis, as this translation does. This is not to say that the Guodian texts do not tell fascinating stories about philosophical ideas circulating in the fourth and third centuries BCE, about the relationship of the *Daodejing* to other texts of the period, including ones that we know about and ones that are new to scholarship, and about the various topics these 'alternate' *Daodejing*s give more or less weight to, but these discussions are best suited to another place.

It will be clear, then, that the question of when the *Daodejing* was written may not be answerable. This is not so much for lack of evidence, but rather because in the very nature of the composition of the book there does not appear to be a single point at which the *Daodejing* could be said to have been completed. The *Daodejing* was almost certainly compiled over a considerable period of time, entering into text (or even texts) at some point long after its aphorisms and verses had circulated orally. The text as we have it today (or something very like it) was, however, clearly established by the late third or early second centuries BCE, as we can see from the Mawangdui texts, as well as from other evidence.

Laozi

The name attached to the *Daodejing* has traditionally been Laozi, literally 'the old master', as was noted above. However, the earliest record we have of him does not appear until about the turn of the first century BCE, in Sima Qian's (?145–?90 BCE) *Historical Records* (*Shiji*). This biography places Laozi as a senior contemporary of Confucius, who himself lived about 400 years earlier than Sima Qian. This span of time has led to doubt being cast on the veracity of the biography. In this record, to add to the confusion, Sima actually identifies Laozi with three different people: one Li Er, known as Li Dan after his death, who was a scribe in the archives of the state of Zhou; a certain Laolaizi who also lived at the time of Confucius; and another man called 'Dan'—written with a different character—who was the grand scribe of Zhou and who was alive in the middle of the fourth century BCE. As Sima himself notes: 'Some say that Dan was Laozi. Others say he was not. Our generation does not know the truth of the matter.'[9]

What is clear is that certain of the features of this biography formed the basis of later stories that grew up around the figure of Laozi. Two of the most important are the interview he had with Confucius and the record of the way the *Daodejing* came into being.

[9] William H. Nienhauser, Jr, *The Grand Scribe's Records: The Memoirs of Pre-Han China by Ssu-ma Ch'ien*, vol. 7 (Bloomington: Indiana University Press, 1994), 23.

In the first, Confucius is said to have gone to Laozi to ask him about the codes of proper behaviour known as the 'rites'. Laozi replied by instructing his visitor that nothing Confucius cared about really mattered and that he should rid himself of his 'arrogant airs', 'many desires', 'contrived posturing', and 'overweening ambition'. Confucius famously observed in response that: 'As for the dragon, I can never know how it mounts the wind and clouds and ascends into the sky. Today I have seen Laozi; is he perhaps like the dragon?'[10] The second element of the biography that proved influential told how Laozi, seeing the decline of the Zhou, decided to depart and headed west. At the pass that led out of the state, the Prefect of the Pass, Yin Xi, asked Laozi to write down his teachings—and this was the *Daodejing*.

As the *Daodejing* became more widely circulated and was taken up by the Daoist religion or the religious movements that were precursors to it in the early centuries of the Common Era, the figure of Laozi became elevated to the status of a deity, as an embodiment of the Way itself, an immortal, or a messiah who would usher in an era of Great Peace. In the second century CE the pivotal text *The Scripture on the Transformations of Laozi* (*Laozi bianhua jing*) proclaimed that Laozi is, himself, 'the root of the Way' and existed before the cosmos came into being.[11] He is a great creator god who became present in the world successively in the form of various sages of antiquity—the teachers of emperors—and who also made appearances in more recent generations. One of the most intriguing aspects of this text is the possibility that it refers to the so-called 'conversion of the barbarians' theory, not long after the introduction of Buddhism to China. This theory has it that when Laozi left through the passes and went west, he continued on until he reached India. There he tried to teach his doctrine to the inhabitants of that land, but they were too slow to grasp it; as a result he taught them an 'easy' version.

---

[10] Ibid. 22.

[11] On the *Laozi bianhua jing*, see Anna Seidel, *La Divinisation du Lao-tseu dans le taoïsme des Han* (Paris: École Française d'Extrême-Orient, 1969). It should be noted that there is a minority opinion that this dating of the text may not be correct.

Those easy teachings are nothing else but Buddhism, and the figure known as the Buddha was none other than one of Laozi's transformations. This theory was not, of course, accepted by Buddhists, and later texts that refer to it much more explicitly than *The Scripture on the Transformations of Laozi* were declared illegal and destroyed under dynasties that were sympathetic to Buddhism.

Not long before *The Scripture on the Transformations of Laozi* was written, we find Laozi deified in early Daoism under the title Lord Lao, the Most High. He was the god who gave revelations to Zhang Daoling, the founder of what became the Celestial Masters sect, in 142 CE granting a new religious dispensation. The Celestial Masters sect is generally regarded as the first organized Daoist Church, in other words, the beginning of the Daoist religion. Under the influence of the various new streams of Daoism in the medieval period, the biography of this, now cosmic and divine, Laozi became much larger and more intricate, and his status in the culture grew in parallel. In the seventh century the Li clan came to power as the Tang dynasty. Since they shared the family name of Li with Laozi—at least according to Sima Qian's biography—they claimed descent from him. Laozi and the *Daodejing*, along with Daoism in general, came to occupy an important place under the Tang, with the *Daodejing* being declared a compulsory text in the official examinations for aspirants to the bureaucracy. The entire text was also inscribed on pillars and stelae in the capital by imperial order, lectures on it were given at court, and in 733 the emperor decreed that a copy of the *Daodejing* should be kept in every home.[12]

The Commentarial Tradition

With the elevation of Laozi into their sponsoring deity, the Celestial Masters also accorded the *Daodejing* a position of honour. A major element in this process was the determination of their own explanation of the book's meaning, known as the *Xiang'er* commentary, which will be discussed below. Commentaries are a

---

[12] See T. H. Barrett, *Taoism Under the T'ang: Religion and Empire During the Golden Age of Chinese History* (London: Wellsweep Books, 1996).

pervasive feature of Chinese scholarly practice. Sometimes explaining the meaning of passages in a text, sometimes providing extracts from other texts that illuminate or are parallel to the passage under examination, sometimes giving information on matters of pronunciation, sometimes noting textual variations in different editions, several commentaries are often found appended to the major works—and occasionally the minor ones—of the Chinese philosophical, historical, and literary traditions. Typically, they are written as interlinear comments: in a traditionally printed Chinese book they appear as half-sized characters interrupting the main text at appropriate points. Some commentaries have become so famous in their own right that other scholars from pre-modern times have written commentaries on them, known as sub-commentaries. Commentaries and sub-commentaries in the Chinese scholarly tradition were not like the notes to an old novel or play we might consult today if we come across a piece of terminology with which we are unfamiliar; rather, they were typically read as an intrinsic part of the text, providing a running interpretation, as well as pointing out references and glossing difficult words.

The *Daodejing*, according to Isabelle Robinet, has been the subject of about 700 commentaries from the third century BCE until the present, by Buddhists and Confucians as well as Daoists—including those of more philosophical bent and those of religious inclination.[13] The fact that the *Daodejing* was not the sole preserve of Daoists is illustrated by the fact that its earliest surviving commentary is found in the book known as *Hanfeizi*, after its author who died in 233 BCE. The *Hanfeizi* is associated with the so-called Legalist school, which was concerned with the preservation of the power of the state through adherence to law and political expediency—yet, perhaps surprisingly to a modern audience, it devotes two chapters to explaining the *Daodejing*.

The three main early commentaries to the *Daodejing* have already been mentioned in this introduction: Heshanggong,

---

[13] Isabelle Robinet, 'Later Commentaries: Textual Polysemy and Syncretistic Interpretations', in Livia Kohn and Michael LaFargue (eds.), *Lao-tzu and the Tao-te-ching* (Albany: SUNY Press, 1998), 119–42, at 119.

Wang Bi, and the *Xiang'er*.[14] In broad terms, Heshanggong, who was probably writing at about the end of the Han dynasty—that is, the late second or early third centuries CE—sees the *Daodejing* in terms of self-cultivation and the need to reduce desires and create harmony and longevity in both the body and the state. In common with much scholarly discussion in his time, Heshanggong is committed to an explanation of the *Daodejing* based on the principles of *yin* and *yang*, and the pervasiveness of *qi* or vital energy in the cosmos. Wang Bi, on the other hand, is generally seen as the main representative of the movement known as Dark Learning, and his reading of the *Daodejing* is focused on philosophical speculations rather than any attempt to find practical instructions in it. For Wang, the Way is not personified, or deified, or capable of intentional action; it is, rather, radically transcendent, the ultimate non-being, the first cause. The third of these commentaries, the *Xiang'er*, was rediscovered only in the twentieth century in a cache of manuscripts found in Dunhuang in the far north-west of China, a stopover on the Silk Route and site of a major Buddhist settlement in medieval times. The part of the commentary that survives— now in the collection of the British Library—only runs from halfway through Chapter 3 to Chapter 37. The meaning of the title *Xiang'er* and when this commentary was written have both been subjects of scholarly discussion and dispute since its discovery. The consensus that seems to be emerging—although there are notable learned dissenters—is that the title means something like 'Thinking of You', which refers to the concern for humanity of the Way, here understood to be essentially identical with the deified Laozi, Lord Lao. The *Xiang'er* belongs to the Celestial Masters tradition that began in the mid-second century CE, and quite possibly derives from the hand of its founder Zhang Daoling's grandson, and great organizer of the movement, Zhang Lu (d. 216).

To better illustrate how very different these three commentaries are, we can compare their interpretations of a certain

---

[14] For an overview of the Heshanggong and Wang Bi commentaries, see Alan K. L. Chan, 'A Tale of Two Commentaries', in ibid. 89–117. The best treatment of the *Xiang'er* is in Stephen R. Bokenkamp, *Early Daoist Scriptures* (Berkeley: University of California Press, 1997), 29–148.

passage in the *Daodejing*, in this case the opening lines of Chapter 6: 'The gully's spirit does not die; She is called "the mysterious cleft".'[15] For Heshanggong, the character 'gully' should be read as 'nourish', and 'spirit' refers to the spirits of the five internal organs; thus, Heshanggong rereads the first line as: 'if you nourish the spirits of the five internal organs you will not die.' He further understands Laozi to mean that the key to not dying lies in the mysterious cleft, with 'mysterious' referring to heaven, and 'cleft' referring to earth. Finally, by relating the cosmos to the human body as macrocosm and microcosm (a standard trope in this period), 'mysterious', which is heaven, refers to the nose, while 'cleft', which is earth, refers to the mouth.

For Wang Bi on the other hand, the spirit of the gully 'is the non-gully within the gully'. He claims that it has no shape and no shadow and it neither opposes anything nor moves around anything. It occupies the lowest position and therefore it is the highest of all things. Nonetheless, since it is so low, Wang says it cannot be given a proper designation: so when Laozi says he 'calls' it the 'mysterious cleft', part of the emphasis is on the verb: as he is unable to define it, he simply gives it a convenient label.

Xiang'er is different again. For its author, the word *gu* that we read as 'gully' should be replaced by a similar character pronounced *yu* that means 'to desire'. Thus, he rereads the first line as meaning 'if you desire that your spirits do not die', and proceeds to give instruction on how to do this. For him, the 'cleft' refers to earth, as it does for Heshanggong, and, by the logic of *yin* and *yang* theory, it is feminine. Man, he says, should follow the feminine and not give himself priority if he wishes to engender internal spirits and keep them alive.

These three readings of the same pair of lines have little in common. Indeed, it would almost appear that the commentators

[15] Discussion of these commentaries is based on the following sources: Heshanggong: Alan K. L. Chan, *Two Visions of the Way: A Study of the Wang Pi and Ho-shang Kung Commentaries on the Lao-tzu* (Albany: SUNY Press, 1991), 139–40; Wang Bi: Rudolph G. Wagner, *A Chinese Reading of the Daodejing: Wang Bi's Commentary on the Laozi with Critical Text and Translation* (Albany: SUNY Press, 2003), 139–40; *Xiang'er*: Bokenkamp, *Early Daoist Scriptures*, 83.

have come to the *Daodejing* with their interpretations already
formed, or that, at least with a little tweaking of the text, they are
able to make the words of the *Daodejing* act as a skeleton on which
they can place the flesh of their choice. This pattern continued
through the history of Chinese commentary on the *Daodejing*,
with new interpretations of it appearing in concert with changes
in the intellectual and religious climate of the times. Indeed, as
Du Daojian observed in the fourteenth century, in an intriguing
echo of the passage from Holmes Welch quoted as the epigraph
to this Introduction: 'Each time the Way has descended to the
earth, it has been different . . . Thus, Han dynasty commentators
produced a Han *Laozi*, Jin commentators produced a Jin *Laozi*,
and Tang and Song commentators produced Tang and Song
Laozis.'[16]

Chinese commentaries on the *Daodejing* did not stop in
medieval times. Indeed, a particularly intriguing example was
written by Yan Fu (1854–1921), one of the greatest transmitters
of western thought to China, and translator of Thomas Huxley,
Adam Smith, John Stuart Mill, Montesquieu, and Herbert
Spencer, the Social Darwinist who coined the term 'survival of
the fittest'.[17] In his marginal notes to the *Daodejing*, Yan found
parallels to aspects of the writings of the authors he was reading
in western languages, in particular to certain elements of
Spencer's philosophy. He also noted echoes of Montesquieu's
prescriptions for a democratic state in the descriptions of Laozi's
ideal society in Chapter 80 of the *Daodejing*, and of Darwinism in
these lines from Chapter 5:

> Heaven and earth are not benevolent:
> They treat the myriad things as a straw dog.

More than a hundred years before Yan Fu had found elements
of western thought in the *Daodejing*, the text had been discovered
by Europeans: several translations into Latin were apparently
made by Jesuits in China during the eighteenth century, one of

---

[16] Chan, *Two Visions of the Way*, 4.
[17] See Benjamin Schwartz, *In Search of Wealth and Power: Yen Fu and the West*
(Cambridge, Mass.: Harvard University Press, 1964).

which was presented to the Royal Society in 1788. The first complete translation into French appeared in 1841 under the name of Stanislaus Julien, and the first into English in 1868 by the Revd John Chalmers, who worked for the London Missionary Society in Hong Kong. Since then translations have appeared regularly—according to Holmes Welch's estimate, between 1934, when Arthur Waley's *The Way and Its Power* appeared, and 1957, when Welch's own *The Parting of the Way* was published, a new translation was produced every sixteen months.[18] After 1957, of course, the *Daodejing* acquired new audiences as one of the required texts of the hippy counter-culture, but this was also the period of increased activity in Chinese Studies in universities across the western world (a still very useful concordance to the text from 1968 is rumoured to have been produced to while away the hours during a student occupation in Munich). As a result, in the 1960s, 1970s, and 1980s the rate of production of *Daodejing* translations undoubtedly increased—and since the occurrence of the Internet, growth in this industry has accelerated.

Tracing the contours of *Daodejing* translation is a mammoth task, and not one that will be attempted here, but some broad outlines can be noted. One of the motivations for the study of the Chinese classics, including the *Daodejing*, in the early period was the attempt to find traces of monotheism in Chinese culture. Some western scholars of China, themselves men of religion, considered that the world had been populated by the scattering of nations after the destruction of the Tower of Babel, as the Jewish Bible narrates. Since this was the case, all peoples at one time must have believed in a single god. If traces of that belief could be found in ancient works from around the world, it would both prove the veracity of Scripture and assist in contemporary missionizing. Even though the word *dao* was rarely actually translated as 'god'—although there are examples of this—the idea that it was singular, was present before the cosmos was formed, and generated all that existed must surely have been persuasive evidence of an ancient Chinese monotheism for people inclined to find it.

[18] Welch, *The Parting of the Way*, 14.

Another frequently encountered motivation for translators of the *Daodejing* is almost the opposite of the first; that is, rather than looking for something familiar in the text, it has been seen as the epitome of the exotic, the storehouse of a wisdom that is radically different from the traditions of the west. These translators proceeded from a position that western culture is, if not moribund, then seriously flawed or corrupt, certainly lacking in a complete understanding of the nature of the cosmos and spirituality. The apparent ambiguity of the *Daodejing* argued, for them, for a stance towards the world in which not all knowledge could be derived with the tools of rationality. Of course, the danger with such a position is that, in the act of translating, either much of this ambiguity disappears or else the text simply becomes incoherent. Ironically, such an anti-rationalist position stood in direct opposition to other western interpretations that maintained that Daoism represented precisely a rationalist position in Chinese philosophy—one well-known translation from 1913 actually translated *dao* as 'reason'.[19]

A third group of *Daodejing* translations finds people approaching the text from already well-established spiritual or religious positions. For them, the *Daodejing* reinforces what they know to be true already. Apart from those people who simply discussed the *Daodejing* in terms of their own philosophy, like Madame Blavatsky, the founder of Theosophy, and the Bhagwan Shree Rajneesh, later known as Osho (the last building he lived in at his ashram in Pune was called Lao Tsu House), a prime example of a 'translation' based on this approach is one by Aleister Crowley, proponent of 'magick' and once called 'the wickedest man in the world'.[20] Writing under the name Ko Hsüan, actually a Daoist immortal of the third century CE, Crowley's 'translation' was first

[19] D. T. Suzuki and Paul Carus, *The Canon of Reason and Virtue* (Chicago: Open Court, 1913). This translation of the title was actually suggested some decades earlier by Samuel Wells Williams, the American missionary, scholar, and diplomat, in volume 2 of his *The Middle Kingdom: A Survey of the Geography, Government, Literature, Social Life, Art and History of the Chinese Empire and its Inhabitants* (New York: Wiley & Putnam, 1848; rev. edn. 1883), in his chapter on the 'Religion of the Chinese'.

[20] Ko Hsüan [Aleister Crowley], *Tao Te Ching* (York Beach: Samuel Weiser, Inc., 1995).

published posthumously in 1971. In it, he blends Hermetic Qabalah with a pre-existing English version of the text. Like many others claiming to have translated the *Daodejing*, Crowley had no knowledge of Chinese, relying instead on the Revd James Legge's version of 1891.[21]

The final category of translations that deserves to be mentioned is, of course, that produced by scholars. These are not limited to works of our time—Legge's, for instance, is most certainly scholarly—but it is true that with the growth in Chinese Studies, and the greater knowledge that has been gained of the nature of ancient China through historical research and philology as well as archaeology, many very fine studies and translations of the *Daodejing* have appeared. This new translation is a case in point. By incorporating insights from the discoveries at Mawangdui and Guodian, and the work of contemporary scholars on many technical questions, Edmund Ryden has produced a *Daodejing* that is not only as learned as any in circulation but also fresh, and sometimes startling, in its rendering.

B. P.

[21] James Legge, *The Texts of Taoism*, Sacred Books of the East (ed. Max Müller), vols. 39 and 40 (Oxford: Clarendon Press, 1891).

NOTE ON THE TEXT AND TRANSLATION

The Chinese editions used as a basis for this translation are *A Concordance to the Daozang Wang Bi ben Laozi and Heshanggong ben Laozi ji Heshanggong zhu*, ed. D. C. Lau and Chen Fong Ching (Hong Kong: Commercial Press, ICS series, 1995) and Liao Mingchun, *Guodian chujian Laozi jiaoshi* (Beijing: Qinghua daxue, 2003). The translation follows that of the classical edited text, corrected where necessary with reference to the ancient versions that have been discovered in recent archaeological excavations (see Introduction, pp. xv-xx).

The classical edited text is known in Chinese as the *Daodejing*, or the *Classic of the Way and the Life Force*. Strictly speaking, this name refers to the text after it has been accepted as 'canonical'. Early versions that may pre-date this 'canonization' of the text may be known as the *Laozi*. However, in practice both appellations are used somewhat indiscriminately, and the two names have become synonymous.

In the Mawangdui versions (see below), the second part in the classical edition seems to come first, and the title is reversed to *Dedaojing*, the *Classic of the Life Force and the Way*.

Readers who know no Chinese will probably also be confused by the various ways in which the Chinese has been transliterated. The current standard international transliteration is the one used here: hence 'the Way' is transliterated as *Dao* and the 'author' is known as Laozi. Older forms of transliteration are still quite common, and the title of the book, *Daodejing*, is also called *Tao-te Ching*, and the 'author' Laozi can be given as Lau-Tzu or Lao Tzu.

The translation is divided into two parts—'The Way' and 'The Life Force'—with eighty-one chapters, numbered according to the classical edition (also referred to as the 'received version'). For reference purposes the chapter numbers of the two principal texts discovered by archaeologists are also included. The first of these sources is a Han dynasty tomb of 168 BCE known as Mawangdui (MWD). In fact the tomb yielded two copies of the *Daodejing* of slightly different date, but in most respects the two are similar and hence we can refer simply to the Mawangdui version, distinguishing the older (A) and newer (B) editions only when they differ. The second archaeological source is a tomb of around 300 BCE, in which three separate bundles of bamboo slips with chapters from the *Daodejing* are recorded. The tomb is at Guodian (GD), and the three bundles are distinguished as A, B, and C, with chapter numbers given by the archaeologists. The chapters are numbered according to the classical edition, followed by the Mawangdui chapter number in brackets. Not all chapters appear in Guodian, but where they do the chapter number is also supplied.

Square brackets [ ] in the translation are used to indicate phrases that are found in the received version but not in the Mawangdui and Guodian versions. These passages may be later additions, such as conjunctions inserted to link verses together, or even notes, which in Chinese style are inserted into the text itself.

Round brackets ( ) indicate phrases found only in the Mawangdui or only in the Mawangdui and Guodian versions. When the *Daodejing* was edited into its current standard form with eighty-one chapters, a number of lines and characters were cut out. The editors presumably wanted a more concise text, but in doing so they sometimes cut so much that the grammar became ambiguous. Hence these passages in round brackets show what was cut out in the process of editing. Complete reconstruction of the original texts of the ancient versions can be found in Henricks, *Lao-tzu's Tao-Te Ching* (see Select Bibliography).

Curly brackets { } indicate phrases found in the received and Mawangdui versions but not in the Guodian version.

Short commentaries intended to elucidate the content of the chapters appear on the opposite pages; further explanatory notes to individual words and phrases can be found at the back of the book, signalled in the text with an asterisk. Three main sources inform the notes: recent scholars (especially D. C. Lau and Wing-tsit Chan); variant readings from the original Chinese editing of the text; and the work done on the Mawangdui and Guodian versions by scholars such as Liao Mingchun, Robert Henricks, and D. C. Lau. The earliest known commentary on parts of the

Daodejing is by Hanfei (*c.*280–*c.*233 BCE), a brilliant philosopher who died tragically young, and the mysterious 'master who lives by the river' (Heshanggong) (between *c.* early fourth century and late sixth century CE), whose verse-by-verse commentary provides the standard moralistic reading of the text.

SELECT BIBLIOGRAPHY

The best-known translation of the *Daodejing* in English is by D. C. Lau, and was published in 1963. Following the publication of the Mawangdui versions Lau revised his translation, publishing it in 1983 in Hong Kong with the Chinese text, and again in 1994 without: D. C. Lau, *Lao Tzu Tao Te Ching: Translation of the Ma Wang Tui Manuscripts* (New York: Alfred A. Knopf, 1994). Another well-known version is by Wing-tsit Chan, and appears in his *Source Book in Chinese Philosophy* (Princeton: Princeton University Press, 1963). Robert G. Henricks has produced a version with detailed notes, and including the Chinese text of the Mawangdui versions: *Lao-tzu: Te-Tao Ching: A New Translation Based on the Recently Discovered Ma-wang-tui Texts* (New York: Ballantine Books, 1989).

To understand the basic metaphors of the Way and of Virtue, there can be no better book than Sarah Allan's *The Way of Water and Sprouts of Virtue* (Albany: SUNY Press), published in 1997 after years of work. Although more technical and speculative, her essay on 'The Great One, Water, and the *Laozi*: New Light from Guodian', *T'oung Pao*, 89: 4/5 (Dec. 2003), 237–85, extends the thought of her book to suggest that the basic metaphor of the Way is that of the Milky Way. Dr Allan also wrote an introduction to the 1994 edition of Lau's translation.

Benjamin Schwartz and Angus Graham have written two very different accounts of Chinese philosophy, both of which deal with the *Daodejing*. Schwartz's *The World of Thought in Ancient China* (Cambridge, Mass.: Harvard University Press, 1985) reads the text as a work of religious, mystical philosophy; whereas Graham's *The Disputers of the Tao: Philosophical Argument in Ancient China* (La Salle: Open Court, 1989) sees it as using logical reversal to upset familiar patterns of speech and recover spontaneity. David Nivison's account of 'The Classical Philosophical Writings' in the *Cambridge History of Ancient China: From the Origins of Civilization to 221 BC* (Cambridge: Cambridge University Press, 1999) places the *Daodejing* in the context of the Legalist philosopher Han Fei, who provides the first commentary on it. All three accounts are worth reading. Max Kaltenmark's *Lao Tzu and Taoism* (Stanford: Stanford University Press, 1969) may be old but is still a good, simple introduction to Laozi, the *Laozi* and Daoism.

Specialists interested in the Guodian text should consult the proceedings of a conference edited by Sarah Allan and Crispin Williams, *The Guodian Laozi: Proceedings of the International Conference, Dartmouth College, May 1998* (Berkeley: Institute for East Asian Studies, University of California, 2000), but this work does not actually give an English translation of the text. On the textual history of the *Laozi*, William Boltz's short but very scholarly account in Loewe's *Early Chinese Texts: A Bibliographical Guide* (Berkeley: Institute of East Asian Studies, 1993) is essential reading.

On early religious Daoism the best introduction is the 'General Introduction' to Stephen R. Bokenkamp's *Early Daoist Scriptures* (Berkeley: University of California Press, 1997). An easily obtained one-volume study is Russell Kirkland's *Taoism: The Enduring Tradition* (New York and London: Routledge, 2004).

Further reading in Oxford World's Classics

Confucius, *The Analects*, trans. Raymond Dawson.
Sima Qian, *The First Emperor: Selections from the Historical Records*, trans. Raymond Dawson.

A CHRONOLOGY OF THE *DAODEJING*

DAODEJING

DARJEELING

THE WAY

The basic metaphor in this chapter is of the Way as the mother who gives life to all that is. What exists comes from the darkness of her womb, but the text stresses that what is visible is the same as what is hidden within the womb. We are invited to think both in the direction of the whole of existence but also to follow life back to its source within the womb. The stripping away of yearning and desire helps us to go back to the womb; whilst allowing full play to yearning makes us long to see all that exists.

I

(MWD 45)

Of ways you may speak,
     but not the Perennial Way;
By names you may name,
     but not the Perennial Name.

The nameless is the inception of the myriad things;*
The named is the mother of the myriad things.

Therefore,
Be ever without yearning* so as to observe her obscurity;
Be ever full of yearning so as to observe what she longs for.*

Both come forth alike and yet are named as opposites,
Alike they are called 'abstruse'.
Abstruse on abstruse, the gate to all obscurity.

Chapter 2 takes us into a world of relative contrasts: hot is hot in relation to cold rather than because there is some absolute heat or coldness. This idea introduces us to the behaviour of the Sage. The Sage is both a wise person and the ruler. Since at the time such a wise ruler was almost certainly male, the translation uses masculine pronouns for the Sage to contrast with the feminine pronouns used for the Way. The Sage is portrayed as someone who does not interfere in the natural course of events. He does not *act*, and as a result things are free to grow and act naturally. The paradox is that precisely by not engaging in deliberate activity, the Sage never loses control.

2

(MWD 46; GD A9)

All under heaven know beauty as beauty, therefore there is
   ugliness;
All under heaven know good as good, therefore there is badness.

[Therefore],
Being and beingless* generate each other;
Difficult and easy form each other;
Long and short shape each other;
High and low complete each other;
Note and voice match each other;
Front and back follow each other.
(Such are all perennial.)

For this reason,
The Sage
     abides in the practice of not acting,
     undertakes teaching without words.

The myriad things act, yet he does not initiate them,*
They generate, yet he does not possess them,*
They act, yet he does not rely on them;
Tasks come to fruition, yet he does not dwell on them.*

Indeed, because he does not dwell on them, for this reason he
   does not lose them.

Our normal expectation is that government officials should be competent persons, but here the Sage is advised to avoid all valuing of things or posts. When a society does not consider things valuable then there will be no competition and people will quietly go about their business, and the astute and clever people will have no means to supplant the ruler.

3

(MWD 47)

Promote not the worthy, then the people will not compete.
Esteem not objects hard to obtain, then the people will not be
  thieves.
Display not what is desirable, then the people's hearts will not
  be turbid.

For this reason,
The government of the Sage is thus:
He empties his mind,* fills his belly;
Weakens his will, strengthens his bones,
Ever making it such* that the people have no knowing, no
  longing.

If you can make it so that the astute dare not act,
Then you will discover there is nothing you cannot govern.

The metaphysical notion of the Way is modelled on the Milky Way. The Milky Way (called Silver River in Chinese) was understood as emerging from the Pole Star. Like all rivers, it flows out of an empty abyss in the mountains (or in the sky). This chapter describes how the Milky Way comes down to earth, as her stars (the sharp points of light) become vague and the light weakens and all is merged with the earth, whilst yet still being the most ancient thing there is. Apart from being seen as a river or as stars, the Way is also like woven cloth, therefore she seems to unravel as she comes closer to earth.

Heshanggong gives a moral reading of the passage, according to which the Sage casts off anger and becomes one with ordinary folk.

4

(MWD 48)

The Way is empty,
Yet in using her, there is something that does not fill her.*
An Abyss
—she is the forebear of the myriad things.

She files away her sharp points;*
She unravels her weft;*
She dims her light;
She merges with the earth.*

Obliterated
—she scarcely exists.
I do not know whose child she is,
—before the first god, she was.

This chapter gives us three sayings which may be unrelated.

The Sage's conduct is modelled on that of heaven and earth, which show no partiality to anyone. The *straw dog* mentioned here was a substitute for a real animal offered in sacrifice. Once the sacrifice was over the model could be discarded.

The second passage on the bellows and blow-pipe is joined to the first because both speak about heaven and earth. Two ideas are brought out: the inexhaustible life of heaven and earth and the fact that their vitality comes from emptiness.

The third saying is perhaps a post-Guodian addition which takes up the theme of emptiness.

5

(MWD 49; GD A12)

Heaven and earth are not benevolent:
They treat the myriad things as a straw dog.
The Sage is not benevolent:
He treats the common people as a straw dog.

Heaven and earth are like the bellows and the blow-tube:*
As emptiness increases, they inhale less and less;*
As they press together, they expel more and more.

{To talk too much is merely chatter;*
It cannot match retaining emptiness.}*

As in Chapter 4, this chapter makes sense if we see the Way as a river, which is what the gully's spirit is; as female, the mysterious cleft is the entrance to her womb; and as woven cloth that continuously comes out from the womb. Weaving was done by women, and among the indigenous tribes of Taiwan men are never allowed to touch the women's looms. The weaver sits on the ground with the loom held by her feet and the cloth emerges as if from her womb. See also the Introduction, pp. xxv–xxvi.

6

(MWD 50)

The gully's spirit does not die;
She is called 'the mysterious cleft'.
The gate to the mysterious cleft
Is called 'the root of heaven and earth'.
Weaving on, continuously existing,
Use of her shall never end.

The Sage models himself on heaven and earth, by putting himself in the last place and so becoming first.

7

(MWD 51)

Heaven grows; earth lasts;
The reason why heaven grows and earth lasts is because
They do not generate themselves;
Therefore they live a long time.

For this reason the Sage
Holds himself back and he is ahead;
Puts aside his self and he exists.

Were this not to be by not valuing his own affairs, how else
    could it be?
Therefore he can accomplish his own affairs.

This chapter lists seven activities, and in each case gives the quality that each activity should aim for. There is a progression from the inner qualities such as thinking towards outward activities which involve governing a state. The last line grants an assurance of success in language reminiscent of the declarations of the diviners recorded on the oracle bones, inscriptions on the shoulder-blades of oxen or turtle plastrons dating from between 1350 and 1100 BCE.

8

(MWD 52)

The highest goodness is like water:
Water benefits the myriad things and rests in the places
   everybody detests.

Therefore,
It is close to the Way.

Dwelling aims to be earth-bound;
Thinking aims to be profound;
Giving aims to be like heaven;*
Speaking aims to be trustworthy;
Governing aims to be correct;
Accomplishing aims to be capable;
Undertaking aims to be timely.

Only through not competing will there be no disaster.

There is a balance in the way of heaven that should be imitated. It imposes a natural control. Four images are suggested: the desire to fill a cup to the brim; to sharpen a sword blade to its finest edge; to accumulate wealth; and to win high position; but all these need to be curtailed if one is to keep to the way of heaven.

9

(MWD 53; GD A20)

To hold and fill is not equal to stopping when nearly full;*
To whet and sharpen a blade means it will not keep for long.
When gold and jade fill* the storeroom,* none can keep them;
When riches and honour lead to pride, you heap disaster on
    yourself.
When tasks are done, then retire, that is the way of heaven.

The poet sets out ways for the ruler to engage in meditation. He is to let
the world be, and in this way alone can he truly govern it. The *earthy soul*
is that aspect of a person that sinks into the ground at death. In meditation
the Sage carries it, as it were, on his head. *Concentrating* qi *to its weakest*:
the image here is masculine: *qi* is the force that flows through the body
and the world, but it is also the male seed, and the idea here is that the
penis is small like that of a baby boy. The birth of a male child represents
the rise of *yang*. *Opening and closing*: here the image is female: the gate
clearly being a reference to the entrance to the womb.

IO

(MWD 54)

Supporting the earthy soul, hugging the One, can you
    ensure they are not lost?
Concentrating *qi* to its weakest, can you be a baby boy?
Washing and cleaning the dark mirror, can you make it
    without stain?
Loving people and giving life to the state,* can you do it
    without knowledge?
Opening and closing heaven's gate, can you do it like a
    woman?
Discerning to the four directions, can you do it without
    knowledge?

She generates them; nourishes them;*
She generates yet does not own them;
She quickens yet does not possess them;
She stewards yet does not master them.

She is called 'abstruse life force'.*

The 'emptiness' at the centre of the wheel or in the pot or the doors and windows is what is most valuable. The frame, the pot, and the spokes simply enclose it. These are all images of the Way within the world.

I I

(MWD 55)

Thirty spokes held in one hub;
—In beingless lies the cartwheel's usefulness;
Moulding clay into pots;
—In beingless lies the pot's usefulness;
Chiselling doors and windows to make a room;
—In beingless lies the room's usefulness;

Therefore,
Possess something to make it profit you;
Take it as nothing to make it useful for you.*

Art, music, tasty food, hunting, and rare objects are all attractive to the eye
and awaken desire. The Sage must learn to say no to these desires.

12

(MWD 56)

The five colours* turn a man's eyes blind;
The five notes turn a man's ears deaf;
The five tastes turn a man's palate dull;
Racing through fields hunting turns a man's heart wild;
Goods hard to obtain cause a man's progress to halt.

For this reason,
The ruling of the Sage* is by the belly not by the eyes.

Therefore,
Reject the latter and take up the former.

Grace (promotion) and *disgrace* (demotion) are granted to a person by the ruler and both come from outside. But how they are seen depends on the reaction of the recipients themselves: this is what is meant by 'honour' and 'dishonour', the subjective evaluation of what has been granted. The poet argues that if we can forget about our own self esteem then it does not matter whether we are promoted or demoted. Such a person has attained to an indifference that makes him a worthy and impartial ruler of the world.

13

(MWD 57; GD B4)

Grace and disgrace strike unexpectedly;
Honour and dishonour are self-inflicted.*

What is meant by grace and disgrace strike unexpectedly?
Grace for those of low estate:
When it comes, comes unexpectedly;
When lost, it is also unexpectedly.
This is what is meant by grace and disgrace strike unexpectedly.

What is meant by honour and dishonour are self-inflicted?
I come across a great disaster because I have a self.
Now, if I did not have a self then what disaster could befall me?

Therefore,
One who values regulating himself as much as regulating the
    world,
May be entrusted with the world.
One who loves himself as much as he loves the world,
May be granted keep of the world.*

In this chapter the images of the Way as starlight (the Milky Way) and as a woven cloth constantly intertwine. The latter image is present in the ideas of 'winding and twisting' and the final reference to *the beginning of the Way*, where the word for beginning refers to the head end of a thread. The image of light is clear from the translation itself.

14

(MWD 58)

Look at her and you do not see her: name her invisible;*
Listen to her and you do not hear her, name her inaudible;
Touch her and you do not feel her, name her intangible.*
These three cannot be investigated further and so they merge
    and become one.
One:* there is nothing brighter above her nor darker below her.

Winding and twisting: she cannot be named;
She reverts back to when there was beingless.
She is called 'the shape without a shape'; 'the image of what is
    not a thing'.
She is obscure light!

Welcoming her* you do not see her head;
Following her you do not see her tail;
Grasping the Way of old* so as to guide the beings of today;
Know that the ancient beginning is called 'the beginning of
    the Way'.

The ideal Way-farer, someone who really puts the Way into practice, is abstruse and profound. He is untouched by civilization and hence seems to be like solid wood or a muddy pool. He is *hun dun*, an expression which refers to the chaos time before the world came to be in its present form: the cosmic soup.

15

(MWD 59; GD A5)

The good Way-farers of olden days were always unseen,
  mysterious, communing with the abstruse, so deep they could
  not be fathomed.
{It is because they could not be fathomed, that,}
Therefore, I make this ode for them:

Careful, as he in winter fords a river;
Cautious, as he fears his neighbours;
Formal, as a guest;
Far off, as apart *as when ice drifts apart*;*
Hun like a wooden lump;*
Dun like a muddy dump.
{Open like a valley.}*

He who can make a muddy pool clear,
It shall then indeed be clear.
He who can make a woman his master,*
She shall then indeed give life.

He who keeps this Way does not want to overflow.

{Only because he does not overflow, can he lie hidden and
  incomplete.}*

The pattern set out here is that of death: returning to the root, stillness, and the allotted length of life. The Mawangdui texts use *heng* as an adverb or adjective referring to what is perennial and *chang* as the noun 'what is ever thus'. The received version obscures the distinction by using *chang* in both cases, in order to avoid the personal name of Liu Heng, Emperor Wen of the Han (r. 180–157 BCE).

16

(MWD 60; GD A13)

Attaining vacuity is perennial;*
Keeping to emptiness is everlasting.*
The myriad things leap forth;*
I am at rest to watch their return.
The heavenly Way* is flourishing;
Each thing returns to its roots.

Returning to the root is called 'stillness';
Stillness, this is called 'returning to life's decree';
Returning to life's decree is called 'what is ever thus';
Knowing what is ever thus is called 'being illuminated';
Not knowing what is ever thus is to be reckless;
Being reckless is to court disaster.
He who knows what is ever thus can embrace all;
He who embraces all can be public-minded;
He who is public-minded can be king;
He who is king can be heaven;
He who is heaven can be the Way;
He who is the Way can last for ever.

By obscuring himself* he never meets disaster.

While no ruler wants to be laughed at, many seek to rule by inspiring fear among their subordinates or by awakening love and respect from their subjects, but the Sage ruler is so unobtrusive that people are hardly aware of his presence and things seem just to happen naturally.

Mawangdui groups Chapters 17–19 as one unit.

17

(MWD 61; GD CI)

Regarding the highest rulers, those below only know of their
  existence;*
As for lesser ones, they love and praise them;
As for even lesser ones, they fear them;
As for the least ones, they mock them.

When trustworthiness is lacking, then there is lack of trust.

Ah-ha! What a valuable saying.
If I complete affairs and achieve my goals,
Then the ordinary people say: 'for us it was just natural.'

In this chapter we learn that the great Confucian moral values of *benevolence*, *justice*, *filial piety*, and *loyalty* are not the highest perfection. The era of the Way itself is much nobler. For more passages criticizing these virtues, see Chapters 19 and 38 below. The six relationships are those between parents and children, older and younger siblings, husband and wife.

18

(MWD 62; GD C2)

Therefore,
When the great Way is neglected there arises benevolence and
  justice;
When wisdom comes forth, there arises great artifice;
When the six relationships are disharmonious, there arises filial
  piety and fraternal affection;
When the state is in chaos, there arises the loyal minister.

This chapter rejects one set of ideals and proposes another. In the received version what is rejected are the Confucian values of benevolence and justice, and of sageliness and wisdom. There is also a rejection of business interests. The Guodian version is weaker: what is rejected are all practices that could fairly universally be condemned: sleight of word in debating, profiteering, and scheming. The ideal proposed is that of simplicity and the termination of desire.

19

(MWD 63; GD A1)

Cut off sageliness,* get rid of wisdom, the people are better off a
hundred times;
Cut off benevolence, get rid of justice, the people return to filial
piety and fraternal affection;
Cut off knavery, get rid of profiteering, thieves and robbers are
no more.

Three sayings, yet their formulation is not sufficient:
Therefore there must be an affirmative injunction:*
Look to the simple; hold the lumpen; reduce self-love; curb
desire.

Learning teaches us what is right and what is wrong, but the *Daodejing* questions whether such distinctions are worthwhile. The poet contrasts himself with those who rejoice and are successful. Even today, Chinese people celebrate the Spring Festival (Chinese New Year) by climbing a terrace to view the countryside.

The Sage of the *Daodejing* is, however, like a stillborn baby. In fact the term is 'stagnant', and moral readings of the 'sign of life' give versions that read *I alone am still, showing no sign of desires*. But if we read it in conjunction with the next line, we see that the baby's smile is the sign of life. He is sucking his mother's milk, literally: *I value eating mother*. In keeping with the above, the image is that of the baby, here sucking its mother's milk, oblivious to all other concerns.

20

(MWD 64; GD B3)

Ending learning brings no sorrow.
Yea and Nay: what does it matter?
Best and Worst: what's the difference?
One whom others fear cannot but fear others too.

Confusion: the end is not yet nigh!
Everyone rejoices,
    as when enjoying a holiday,
    or when in Spring one climbs a terrace.*
I alone am stillborn, showing no sign of life,
Like a baby that has not yet smiled.
Wearied: I have nowhere to go to.

Everybody has more than enough and I alone am bereft.
I have a fool's heart, dull, dumb.

Common folk shine; I alone am gloomy;
Common folk excel; I alone am downcast.
Adrift like the sea, blown about with nowhere to halt.
Everyone has good reasons; I alone have a bumpkin's
    stubbornness.

I long to be alone and am unlike others, for I appreciate
    sucking my mother's milk.

This chapter develops the maternal image of the Way, which I have brought out in the translation by using the term 'womb'. The sequence of the lines takes us back from the vague embryo to the seed that first brought about the pregnancy.

21

(MWD 65)

That utmost life force* includes all things is only because it
    comes from the Way.
The Way is without action: uniquely vague, uniquely elusive.
Elusive ah! Vague ah! Within her womb there is a vague shape.
Vague ah! Elusive ah! Within her womb there is a something.
Recess ah! Obscure ah! Within her womb there is the seed.
That seed is most authentic.* Within her womb it is sure.
From of old till now, her name does not fade.

By this we observe the emergence of all things.*
How do I know the shape of the beginning of all things?
By this.

In the Mawangdui versions the order of the next four chapters is 24–22–23–25.

22

(MWD 67)

Only by bending can you be whole;
Only by twisting* can you be straight.

Only by hollowing out can you be full;
Only by being used up* can you be new.

Only by reducing can you obtain;
Only by having excess can you be tempted.

For this reason,
The Sage embraces the One so as to be the pointer of all under
    heaven.*
He does not reveal himself,* therefore he shines brightly;
He does not affirm himself; therefore he radiates out;
He does not appropriate to himself, therefore he achieves.
He does not magnify himself, therefore he increases.

It is only because he does not compete that, therefore, under
    heaven there is none who can compete with him.*
The old saying *Only by bending can you be whole* is very true.*

Truly it enables one to go home to wholeness.

The initial metaphors make clear that everything only lasts for a certain period of time; there is a time of growth and a time of loss and both are aspects of the Way. Some translations associate only the time of growth with the Way and assume that the time of loss refers to losing the Way, but such a reading does not fit the grammar or structure of the passage. The words for *life force* and *knife force* sound alike in ancient Chinese and even in some older dialects today.

23
(MWD 68)

Silent of speech is nature's course.
Therefore a typhoon does not last all morning;
Pounding rain does not last all day.
Who makes them? Heaven and earth.*
Yet if heaven and earth cannot make them last,
Then how much less can men do so?

Therefore,*
For one who acts according to the Way:
The Way-farer becomes one with the Way:
The grower becomes one with the life force.
The loser becomes one with the knife force.

For one who is one with the Way, the Way likewise is happy
   to have him;
For one who is one with the life force, the life force likewise is
   happy to have him;
For one who is one with the knife force, the knife force
   likewise is happy to have him.

[When trustworthiness is lacking, then there is lack of trust.]*

24

(MWD 66)

The puffed up* do not stand upright;
The overleaping do not walk ahead;

The self-revealing* do not shine brightly;
The self-affirming do not radiate out;

The self-appropriating do not achieve;
The self-magnifying do not increase.

With respect to the Way these are called 'over-eating
    and overdoing it'.
As there are things that hate this,

(Therefore,)
Those who have the Way* do not indulge in them.

This chapter, along with Chapters 1, 40, and 42, is one of the great metaphysical chapters of the *Daodejing*. The Way is transcendent to all that exists. No language can be adequate to describe her. The only name that is appropriate is 'great'. The title the 'Way' is the public designation and not a personal name. The text explains 'great' as going far away and then returning, clearly an image of the sun, which seems to go far away at sunset but next morning comes back. However, this does not mean the Way is the sun. It simply means that the image of the sun's cycle is one picture conjuring up the sense of surpassing greatness.

The metaphysics of the *Daodejing* is a political metaphysics. The king embodies the Way and is hence great, just as heaven and earth are. In pre-imperial China the Zhou king was the nominal ruler of all China, though the term 'king' was also used in the southern state of Chu and later by usurping states in the north. Use of the royal title involved a political-religious claim: the ruler sees himself as the centre of the world for his state is like the Way is to the world.

25

(MWD 69; GD A11)

A thing* was formed murkily; she was generated before heaven
and earth.
Silent and vast,* unique she stands and does not change;
She turns full circle and is not used up.*
She can be the mother of the world.*

I do not know her name; I entitle her* the Way;
I force myself to name her Great.
What is great goes afar; going afar she turns, turning she
comes back.
The Way is great,* heaven is great, earth is great, and the King
is also great.

In the realm there are four greats and the King is one of them.
Humans imitate the earth; earth imitates heaven;
Heaven imitates the Way; the Way imitates her natural self.*

This chapter describes the Sage ruler who is not distracted by everything happening around him, but in the calm of his own home is able to be one with the Way and hence see beyond and more deeply into reality without being misled by superficial events. He must keep to the root, to the basic Way, and only then can he wield power over the world.

26

(MWD 70)

Heaviness provides the root for what is light;
Stillness wields her sceptre over what is noisy.

For this reason,
The Sage travels all day and does not leave his wagon-train.*
Only when* in his gate tower* at rest, does he see beyond.

How is it that the lord of ten thousand chariots can so lightly
 scorn the world?

Were he light then he would fall away from the root;
Were he noisy then he would fall away from the sceptre.

The five images that open this chapter all suggest that the Sage acts in such a way as to leave no trace of his passing. This idea has already been encountered in Chapter 17. The second part of the chapter notes that nothing and no one are to be rejected.

27

(MWD 71)

The good traveller leaves no cart rut;
The good speaker is flawless in his admonition;
The good accountant uses no marker or slip;

The good closer of doors uses no bolt or bar, yet the doors
    cannot be opened;
The good binder of knots uses no string or rope, yet the knots
    cannot be undone.

For this reason,
The Sage is
Always good at saving people, therefore there is no one left out;
Always good at saving things, therefore there is nothing left out.

This is called 'Wearing Insight upon Insight'.*

Therefore the good person is the teacher of the bad;
The bad person is the raw material for the good.
If you do not value your teacher or if you do not love your raw
    material,
Then even if you are wise yet you will go greatly astray.

This is called 'the Key to the Mystery'.

Here we have three contrasting pairs: cock–hen, white–black, glory–shame. The conspicuous roles are what most desire: the pride of the cock, the purity of whiteness, and the glory of a high position. These must all be known, but the Sage is to aim for their opposites: the inconspicuous submissiveness of the hen, the impurity of blackness, and the shame of a low position, because only in this way can he attain to simplicity.

28

(MWD 72)

To know the cock yet hold on to the hen is to be the valley of
the world.
Once you are the valley of the world, perennial life force will not
desert you.
Perennial life force not deserting you brings you back to the
state of the infant.

To know the white yet hold on to the black is to be the pointer
of the world.
Once you are the pointer of the world, perennial life force will
not waver.
Perennial life force not wavering brings you back to the
limitless.

To know honour* yet hold on to shame is to be the gully of the
world.
Once you are the gully of the world, perennial life force will
now suffice;
Perennial life force now sufficing brings you back to lumpen
wood.

Lumpen wood is cut up and made into cups;
The Sage uses it,* however, to become the chief official.

Therefore,
Great ruling leaves no scar.

The Sage has nothing to do with extremes, whether good (excellence) or bad (excess).

29

(MWD 73)

There are those who want to take the world and run it:
   I see they will not succeed.
The world is a spiritual vessel and cannot be run.
One who runs it destroys it; one who seizes it loses it.

Therefore for things:
     Some go ahead; some follow behind;
     Some blow hot; some blow cold;
     Some are strong; some are conquered;
     Some file down; some are filed down.

For this reason,
The Sage rejects extremes,
             rejects excess,
                  rejects excellence.

Chapters 30 and 31 deal with warfare. China has no tradition of pacifism, but there is much discussion of the morality of warfare. Conflict was seen as inevitable, and great Sages even engaged in conflict to bring about justice. The Tang dynasty general Wang Zhen wrote a commentary on the *Daodejing* in a pacifist sense, urging the emperor, Xian Zong (r. 805–20) to reduce warfare.

In this chapter the focus is on the attitude of the commanding general. Indeed, the greatest general is the one who can succeed without ever a battle being fought.

30

(MWD 74; GD A4)

One who helps the lord of men according to the Way,
Does not use arms to subdue the world since such actions
    easily rebound.
Where armies are encamped, thorny bushes grow.
[After great battles there will inevitably be lean years.]*

The good know when enough is enough and do not go on
    to win subjection.*

When enough is done he does not boast of it;*
When enough is done he does not brag about it;
When enough is done he does not take pride in it.*

[Even that enough is done only as a last resort.]

This is called
'Doing enough and not going on to subdue.'

When things are mature* then they turn old: this is called
    'Negating the Way'.
What negates the Way will soon be lost.

In the Han dynasty, Liu An, king of Huainan (*c.* 179–122 BCE), supervised a compilation of pre-Han thoughts on many subjects. Chapter 15 of his *Huainanzi* takes up the theme of warfare and describes the general leaving the temple to go to war dressed as if he were a corpse. On returning victorious he offers his apologies for the slaughter and retires.

31

(MWD 75; GD C4)

Now as for weapons, they are instruments of bad luck;
Such things: there are those that hate them;
Therefore those who have the Way do not dwell on them.

The Gentleman
    when at peace appreciates the left;
    when at war appreciates the right.

For this reason it is said:

Weapons are instruments of bad luck;
They are not the instruments of a gentleman.

Only as a last resort may they be used.
Even then, concealing sharp edges* is the priority,
They should not be indulged in.*

To indulge in them is to enjoy slaughtering others.
Now one who enjoys slaughtering others cannot realize his
   will in the world.

Therefore,
On festive occasions the left is the place of honour;
At funerals the right is the place of honour.*

For this reason,
The lieutenant-general stands on the left;
The commander-in-chief stands on the right.
In other words, they take position as at a funeral.

Therefore,
When others are slaughtered in numbers, weep over it with
   sorrow and grief;
When victory is won, mark it with a funeral ceremony.

While the Way is named 'great', she is also small. As this chapter shows, she is like a little stream in a valley, but the stream will become the river and the ocean and hence it is both small and great at the same time.

32
(MWD 76; GD A10)

The Way is ever nameless,
When lumpen she seems small,
Yet heaven and earth do not dare to treat her as their
  subordinate.

If counts* and kings could grasp her,
The myriad things would pay court to them of themselves.

Heaven and earth came together to send down sweet dew
—Though none among the people commanded them—
They spread it evenly by themselves.

Once a beginning was determined, there were names.
Once there were names,
Then you must also know them;
If you know them you will be able to avoid disaster.*

The Way is to the world, as a small gully is to rivers and seas.*

33

(MWD 77)

To know others is wisdom;
To know oneself is insight.

To conquer others is to have force;
To conquer oneself is to be strong.

To know what is enough is to be rich;
To forcibly press on is to be ambitious.

To not lose what one has is to last;
To die yet not depart* is to be long-lived.

This chapter again brings us to reflect on the paradox of the Way as both great and small. The image of water that is clear, from the first line, can help us to also understand the rest of the chapter: water enters into all things but does not claim lordship over them: rather, it enables them to grow and be themselves. The Sage is asked to carry out a similar role.

34

(MWD 78)

The great Way floods her banks; she can go left or right.

She completes her tasks, pursues her affairs, yet she is given no
ownership for this.
The myriad things flow back to her, yet she does not lord it over
them,*
On the contrary,
She is ever without yearning and can be named among the small
things.
The myriad things flow back to her, yet she does not lord it over
them,
She can be named among what is great.

For this reason,
The reason why the Sage can do great things is because he never
himself acts as great,
Therefore he can be great.

The Way lacks attraction and so most people ignore her, but the Sage knows better.

35

(MWD 79; GD C3)

Model yourself on* the great symbol, and the world will turn
    to you.
All will turn to you and be unharmed, thus there will be great
    peace.
For entertainment and refreshments, passing travellers will halt.

Therefore,
The discourse of the Way* is insipid and tasteless:
Looking at her, you will not see her;
Listening to her, you will not hear her,
Yet she cannot be used up.*

A series of four paradoxes culminates in the idea of the weak overcoming the strong. The final metaphor contrasts fish and weapons. Both fish and armour have scales, so the fish is a symbol of the Sage, who is the secret weapon of a state.

36

(MWD 80)

If you want to shrink something, you must definitely stretch it;
If you want to weaken something, you must definitely
    strengthen it.
If you want to abolish something, you must definitely elevate it;*
If you want to snatch something, you must definitely donate it.

This is called 'Subtle Insight'.
What is weak and soft wins out over what is hard and strong.

A fish should not be withdrawn from the deeps;
The sharp weapons of the state should not be shown to others.

37

(MWD 81; GD A7)

The Way is ever nameless.
[And so there is nothing she does not do.*]
If counts and kings could grasp her, then the myriad things
    would act* of their own accord.
If they act and want to impel,
Let them* correct* things on the pattern of the nameless lump.
They will also know what is enough.*
To know what is enough enables one to comprehend.*
The myriad things will fix themselves* of their own accord.

THE LIFE FORCE

In the Mawangdui versions this is Chapter 1 of the text. It is also the first chapter commented on by Hanfei. The chapter opens the traditional second part, the *Dejing* (Classic of the Life Force). Along with Chapter 19, it sees the Confucian values as a falling-away from the values of the Way.

38

(MWD 1)

The highest life force does not cling to vitality, for this reason it
   is vital;
The lowest life force does not let go of vitality, for this reason it
   has no vitality;

The highest life force neither acts nor has any motive to do so.
[The lowest life force acts, yet it has a motive to do so;]*
The highest benevolence acts, but still it has no motive to do so.
The highest justice both acts and has a reason to do so.
The highest ceremony acts, and if none respond, it rolls up its
   sleeves and forces them.

Therefore,
Once the Way was lost, only then was there the life force;
Once the life force was lost, only then was there benevolence;
Once benevolence was lost, only then was there justice;
Once justice was lost, only then was there ceremony.

This ceremony is the veneer of loyalty and trust and the ugly
   head of disorder.
To be acquainted with this beforehand is the blossoming of the
   Way and the first step to becoming a fool.

For this reason, the Great Man
Abides in the substance, and does not dwell in the veneer;
Abides in the fruit, and does not dwell in the flower.

Therefore,
Reject the latter and choose the former.

The unique is another name for the Way but it is also a political claim: the unique ruler has absolute claims over his state. The Way enables things to realize their true essence and hence is the basis for political rule.

39

(MWD 2)

Those of old who grasped the unique are the following:

Heaven grasped the unique and became clear;
Earth grasped the unique and became still;
Spirits grasped the unique and became ghostly;
Gullies grasped the unique and became full;
[The myriad things grasped the unique and became alive;]
Counts and kings grasped the unique and became the norm for
the world.

The sequel of this is:
It is said: had heaven not been clear, then, I fear, it would have split;
It is said: had earth not been still, then, I fear, it would have
crumbled;
It is said: had spirits not been clear, then, I fear, they would
have ossified;
It is said: had gullies not been full, then, I fear, they would have
run dry;
[It is said: had the myriad things not become alive, then, I fear,
they would have perished;]
It is said: had counts and kings not esteemed rank, then, I fear,
they would have fallen.

Therefore,
Nobility is rooted in humility; high rank is founded in lowliness;

For this reason,
Counts and kings call themselves Orphan, Widower, Lack-Grain.*

Is this not to be rooted in humility? Is it not?

Therefore,
They consider their army of chariots as having no chariot.*

Wherefore,
Seek not to jingle-jingle like jade pendants,
Rather rumble-rumble like huge boulders.*

Another of the metaphysical chapters. We have already seen that the greatness of the Way is defined in terms of a reversal, characterized by the movement of the sun with respect to the earth. Weakness is a characteristic of water and hence also of the Way. What makes this chapter famous is its sequence of 'beingless' to 'being' to 'all that exists'. Each is said to generate the next, where the verb 'generate' is that of plant growth. In other words the basic image is of a seed generating a sapling, which becomes a tree. There is a continuity of movement that is obscured if we take beingless and being as separate objects.

It is instructive to see how the two most famous early commentaries read this chapter.

Heshanggong comments: 'Heaven and earth, spirits bright, insects that fly and worms that wriggle all are generated from the Way. The Way is without form, hence it is said to be generated from nothing. This saying indicates that the root is more important than the flower, weakness more powerful than strength, humility overcomes pomposity.'

Wang Bi writes: 'Things under heaven all are generated through being. What being begins from is by taking beingless as its root. If you want to attain to the fullness of being, you must return to beingless.'

Since we cannot be sure of the date of the Heshanggong commentary it is not clear which of these two is earlier, but their joint existence gave rise to continuous discussions, with philosophers generally preferring Wang Bi.

In the Mawangdui versions this chapter is found after the next (Chapter 41).

40

(MWD 4; GD A19)

Reversal is the moving of the Way;
Weakness is the using of the Way.
The world's myriad things are generated from being;
Being is generated from beingless.

Only a few people understand the importance of the Way. Many simply laugh at it. From this observation the poet goes on to list various paradoxes associated with the Way or the Life Force (here translated as 'vitality'). The chapter ends with four cryptic lines. The Great Square is the symbol of earth, which was portrayed as square in some early Chinese cosmological models. By definition, a square has four corners, but earth is 'great' and hence more than the model which represents it, so it has no corners. The finished shape of an object is what defines what it is: a cup, a bowl, for instance; but the universe itself is never completed and so has no final shape. The other two paradoxes function in the same way: one in the realm of sound and one in the realm of visible images. All these are great and hence surpass fixed definitions and names. The Way is also like this.

41

(MWD 3; GD B5)

Top officials hear the Way: they can (hardly)* fare by her.
Average officials hear the Way: parts they keep; parts they lose.
Low officials hear the Way and greatly mock her.
Were there not this great mockery,*
She could not be good enough to be the Way.

Therefore,
A proverb puts it:

Bright Way looks obscure;
Forward Way looks reversed;
Smooth Way looks rough.*

Utmost vitality looks like a gully;
Great purity looks filthy;
Expansive vitality looks inadequate;
Affirmative vitality looks insouciant;
Substantive authenticity looks unstable.

The great square has no corners;
The great completion is not completed;
The great note has no voice;
The great symbol has no shape.

The Way is great* yet nameless.
The Way alone is good at inaugurating and then completing
    things.*

The identity of the *Unique*, *Double*, and *Triplet* (literally One, Two, and Three) has exercised many minds. Wang Bi says that the Unique is non-being and the Double is being and both together they are the Triplet. The Double could also be heaven and earth or *yin* and *yang*, which are mentioned in this chapter, one of the rare occurrences of a pair which later came to dominate Chinese philosophy. Indeed, if we read the terms in the context of this chapter alone, it would seem that the Unique is another name for the Way, the Double is *yin–yang*, and the Triplet is *qi*.

42

(MWD 5)

The Way generates the Unique;
The Unique generates the Double;
The Double generates the Triplet;
The Triplet generates the myriad things.
The myriad things recline on *yin* and embrace *yang*
While vacuous *qi* holds them in harmony.

What people hate is none other than being an orphan, a
    widower, or lacking grain,
Yet kings and dukes take these as their titles.

Therefore,
Among things: some are decreased by being increased,
And some are increased by being decreased.

Therefore,
What others teach, I also teach.

Therefore,
A strong pillar does not die a natural death.
I will take this as the father of my teaching.

43

(MWD 6)

The softest thing in the world* canters over the hardest thing in
  the world;
That-which-is-not enters where there is no crack.

By this I know the benefit of not acting.

Wordless teaching, the benefit of not acting:
There are few in the world who attain to it.

The sayings in this chapter all take up the theme of avoiding excess.

44

(MWD 7; GD A18)

Reputation or self: which is more desirable?
Self or possessions: which is more valuable?
Gain or loss: which is more a hindrance?

[Wherefore,]
Extreme love leads to great waste;
Much hoarding leads to much loss.

(Therefore,)
If you know what is enough you will not be shamed;
If you know when to stop, you will not perish.
It will be possible to last for long.

As in Chapter 41, what is great is never defined and finished but because it is great it is also never used up. The images derive from the everyday world, but all suggest the transcendence of the Way.

45

(MWD 8; GD B7)

Great achievement seems to lack:
Yet its use has no end.

Great fullness seems empty:
Yet its use has no limit.

Great straightness seems bent;*
Great skill seems clumsy;
Great eloquence seems tongue-tied.

Exercise conquers cold; stillness conquers heat.
If you can be calm and still, you can be the governor of the world.

The first contrast here is between having the presence and absence of the Way. Lack of the Way implies war and disorder.

One of the causes of war listed in ancient Chinese books on war is the desire for profit, so it is not surprising that the next section returns to the idea of being satisfied with what one has, avoiding desire for gain, as in Chapter 44.

46

(MWD 9; GD A3)

When the world has the Way, trotting horses are used for their
  dung;
When the world lacks the Way, war-horses are born on temple
  mounds.*

(There is no graver crime than wanting too much;)
There is no bigger disaster than not knowing what is enough;*
There is no greater misfortune than wanting to get.

{Therefore,}
To know that enough is enough, this is ever to have enough.

In Chapter 26 we have already seen that the Sage shuts himself off from the mundane world and becomes one with the Way and hence truly knows. The First Emperor of Qin tried to put this into practice and ruled from a secret room in a vast palace. However, he is better known for his harsh laws and cannot be said to have truly grasped the Way.

47
(MWD 10)

Go not out the door, know all under heaven;
Peep not out the window: see the way of heaven.
The further away you go the less you know.

For this reason,
The Sage
    walks not, yet knows,
    sees not, yet names;
    acts not on things, yet they are completed.

In Chapter 20 we saw that learning is a matter of distinguishing various things; but the true Way-farer seeks rather to unlearn and come to a point of quiet. Only then can he rule the world.

48

(MWD II; GD B2)

A person given to studies makes daily progress;
A person given to the Way makes daily regress.
Regress and again regress, until coming to not acting.
When not acting then there is nothing not done.

If you acquire the world, ever be without anything to do.
Should there be something to do,* one is not up to acquiring the
    world.

The Sage is like the Way in not imposing on the world.

49

(MWD 12)

The Sage has no fixed mind: he takes the people's mind
    as his mind.

The good ones I value; the not good ones I also value,
Therefore I win* goodness;
The trustworthy ones I trust; the untrustworthy ones
    I also trust,
Therefore I win trust.

The Sage joins with the world,
And with the world he merges his mind.*
The common people all fix their ears and eyes on him:*
The Sage treats them all as his children.

Tradition has bequeathed us two ways of translating the opening of this chapter. The problem lies in the expression *three ten*. The most logical sense is to read it as *three in ten* and assume it means 'one third'. Reading this way, the chapter refers to people as one third devoted to life, one third to death, and one third who make such an effort to pursue life that they too die. The chapter can then be read as stressing the need to avoid a forced pursuit of life as it can only lead to premature death.

A more grammatically correct reading of the phrase is as *thirteen*. Indeed, the earliest commentary on the passage in the *Hanfeizi* read it this way. But this leaves us wondering what the thirteen are in each case.

50

(MWD 13)

We come out into life and enter into death:
Life's adherents are one third;
Death's adherents are one third.

People who strenuously pursue life,
By their activities, are [likewise] one third adherents of death.
Why is this so?
Because they strenuously pursue life.

Perhaps you have heard about those who are good at keeping
    hold of life:
They walk on land and do not meet rhinos* or tigers;
Joining the army they do not wear armour or carry weapons.

The rhino finds no place to stick its horn;
The tiger finds no place to sink its claws;
Weapons find no place to catch their blade.

Why is this so?
Because there is no place for death in them.

51

(MWD 14)

The Way generates them and the life force nourishes them;
Material embodies them and the final shape* completes them.

For this reason,
Among the myriad things [there is none]*
That does [not] honour the Way and appreciate the life force;

The honour paid to the Way and the appreciation owed the
    life force,
Is not like the bestowal* of honours
But is ever according to what is so of itself.

Therefore,
The Way generates them* and nourishes them;
She grows them and raises them;
She determines them and settles them;
She nurtures them and protects them.

She
Generates and does not possess them;
Acts and does not rely on them;
Grows and does not lord over them.*

She is called 'abstruse life force'.

This chapter has three sections. In the first we learn that just as by understanding the mother we can know her children, so it is we understand what exists by knowing the Way. The second, found both here and in Chapter 56, tells us to go back to silence, away from the world, whilst the final section stresses the paradoxical nature of insight and strength, born from this return to the mother and to silence.

52

(MWD 15; GD B6)

The world was conceived, by she who is the mother of the
world.
If you can attain the mother then you will know her child;
If you know her child then you can go back and cling to its
mother.
Then for your whole life you will have no disaster.

Bolt your ears; plug your mouth:*
All life long you shall not fall ill.

Open your mouth; plunge into your affairs:
All life long you shall not be well.*

To see what is small is called 'insight';
To keep to what is weak is called 'strength'.

Use what light there is to return, go back to insight;
You will not abandon yourself to disaster:
This is called 'Putting into Practice what is ever thus'.

While water is the dominant image used for the Way, that of a road is not absent. Here we find the Way is the straight and level road in contrast to tortuous mountain paths. The contrast provides a context to the following description of the luxurious life of courtiers, here condemned as robbery.

53

(MWD 16)

If I had only little knowledge,
When walking on the highroad, I would but fear to go astray.
The highroad is level yet the people like mountain paths.*

Courts are free of weeds, while fields are overrun with darnel.
Granaries are empty, while robes are embroidered silk.

Bearing sharp swords; feasting on drink and food;
Riches in excess: this is called 'rapacious extravagance'.
'Rapacious extravagance': such is not the Way, oh no!

There are five levels of society described here: the individual person, the family, village, state, and the whole world. Each has its own intrinsic independence and so should be seen only in its own context.

54

(MWD 17; GD B8)

What is well established cannot be uprooted;*
What is well protected* cannot be removed.

The descent of children and grandchildren
Is maintained by their rituals* and so is unending.

By practising it in oneself, one's vitality is truly correct.*
By practising it in one's family, one's vitality has a surplus.
By practising it in one's district, one's vitality will grow.
By practising it in one's country, one's vitality will blossom.
By practising it in the world, one's vitality will be universal.

Therefore,
By what is proper to the self observe the self;
By what is proper to the family observe the family;
By what is proper to the district observe the district;
By what is proper to the country observe the country;
By what is proper to the world observe the world.

How may I then know the world as it is?

By this.

Daoist meditation techniques stress returning to the state of a child, to breathe as a child does in the womb and, here, to grasp the paradox that a weak child will live longer than a strong man, since the latter is nearer death.

55
(MWD 18; GD A17)

One who keeps the fullness of the life force,
Is comparable to a newborn child.

Wasps, scorpions, adders, and kraits* do not sting him;
Fierce beasts do not seize him; birds of prey do not grasp him.*
His bones are supple, sinews soft, yet he grasps firmly.

He does not yet know the harmony of female and male yet his
    penis* is aroused:
The epitome of essence!

All day long he shouts and yet is not hoarse.
The epitome of harmony!*

To know harmony is called 'what is ever thus';
To know what is ever thus is called 'insight';
To block life* is called 'inauspicious';
The mind controlling *qi* is called 'strengthening'.

When things are at their peak they grow old.
This is called 'Lacking the Way'.*

{What is lacking the Way dies early.}*

The Way is beyond speech, beyond the grasp of the senses, and untouched by the evaluations we may make of her, whether of praise or blame.

56

(MWD 19; GD A15)

One who knows her does not speak of her;
One who speaks of her does not know her.

Plug your mouth; bolt your ears:*
Dim the light, unite with the dust;*
File your sharp points, unravel your weft.

This is called
'Becoming one with the abstruse'.

Therefore,
You may neither befriend her, nor may you distance her;
You may neither reward her, nor may you harm her;
You may neither honour her, nor may you dishonour her.

Therefore,
She earns the world's appreciation.

Although the Legalist school developed the idea of the Law as the visible embodiment of the Way, Chinese tradition remains suspicious of law. Confucians believed that people who lived virtuously would not have recourse to law, whilst the Daoists maintained that if the natural course of things was followed, as recommended in this chapter, the law would be a hindrance rather than a help.

57
(MWD 20; GD A16)

Use orthodox methods to govern a state;
Use stratagems to manoeuvre armies;
Use doing nothing to gain the world.

How do I know that this is so? By this:

Now,
When heaven* issues many prohibitions and ordinances,
Then the people are more likely to revolt.*
When the people have more sharp weapons,
Then the state is disordered.
When others have more cunning and tricks,
Then strange things arise.
When laws and commands are promulgated,
Then brigands and robbers will be more.

For this reason
The words of the Sage say:*
>   I do not act yet the people act* of themselves;
>   I appreciate examining yet the people are correct* of
>   themselves;
>   I do not interfere yet the people become rich of
>   themselves;*
>   I long to be without longing,* yet the people are lumpen of
>   themselves.

Following on from the previous chapter, we see that the ideal state does not interfere, it allows the people to be simple; if it does make complicated laws then the people become skilled at getting round them. The chapter then includes a number of paradoxical sayings, designed to make us stop and think.

The scholar Jia Yi (201–169 BCE) had been sent down in disgrace from the court and wrote his famous 'Owl Poem' in Changsha, the town where the Mawangdui tombs are. In this poem he reflects on the instability of life—all things change—and quotes the second stanza of this chapter: 'Disaster ah! Fortune's head-rest; Fortune ah! Disaster's back-rest.'

58

(MWD 21)

Administration bumble-humble; people simple-simon.
Administration nitty-picky; people* wheeling-dealing.

Disaster ah! Fortune's head-rest;
Fortune ah! Disaster's back-rest.

Who knows their limit? Is there nothing orthodox?
Orthodox reverts to strange; good reverts to monstrous.

Humans being misled is attested from of old.

For this reason,*
    Be square but do not cut.
    Be angular but do not poke.
    Be straight but do not force.*
    Be bright but do not dazzle.

Just as agriculture depends on storing the harvest, so too the Sage rules by
storing vitality and hence is strong enough to face adversity.

59

(MWD 22; GD BI)

In governing others and serving heaven, there is nothing like
    storing.
Such storing is achieved through prior collecting.*
Prior collecting is called 'Doubling the Accumulation of
    Vitality'.

If you double the accumulation of vitality, there is nothing you
    cannot overcome.
When there is nothing you cannot overcome, none can know
    your limits.
When none can know your limits, then you can possess a
    country.
When you have the country, concentrate on the essentials,* you
    can endure for long.

This is called:
'The Way of being deeply rooted, firmly entrenched, long lived,
    caring for ever.'

The opening proverb of this chapter is justly famous. The little fish remain whole throughout the cooking, so too the Daoist Sage does not damage the state he rules.

60

(MWD 23)

Governing a large country is like steaming small fish.

When you employ the Way to approach the world,
Ghosts will have no spirit.
Or rather it is not that ghosts have no spirit, it is that their spirit
cannot harm people.
In fact, it is not that their spirit cannot harm people, it is also
that the Sage does not harm people.

Since neither does them any harm,
Therefore,
Their life forces intermingle and come back to them.*

While the Warring States period is noted for the rise of one state, Qin, to the exclusion of all others, here the relationship of large and small states is seen as complementary, as the union of male and female. This depicts a more ideal relationship than what in fact came to happen with Qin's direct annexation and obliteration of the smaller states.

61

(MWD 24)

A great state is like a river's lower course,
She is the feminine aspect of the world.

In the mating of the world:
The feminine always conquers the masculine by stillness.
It is because of her stillness that she is apt to take the lower
    position.*

Therefore,
When a great state is below a small state,
Then she shall take over the small state.
When a small state is below a great state,
Then she shall be taken over* by the great state.

Therefore,
The one is below so as to take over; the other is below and so is
    taken over.

Therefore,
The great state desires none other than to embrace and feed
    people,*
The small state desires none other than to enter in and serve
    people.*
Now for both to obtain what they desire, then the greater is
    fittingly below.

This chapter argues that the Way is what is most valuable in the world, a
fitting gift to be offered to one's overlord.

62

(MWD 25)

The Way is
The reservoir* of the myriad things;
The treasure of good people;
The protector of bad people.

Eloquent speech can be used for bargaining;
Fawning* conduct can be used for bribing* others.

Though people treat something as not good, why reject it?

Therefore,
When the Son of Heaven is enthroned and the Three
   Ministers* placed,
Rather than offering them jade disks followed by* teams of
   four horses,
Sit down and offer this.*

Why was this appreciated of old?
Was it not said:
'By her one seeks and obtains;
Should one have committed a crime,
By her one avoids punishment.'

Therefore,
It is valued by the world.

The initial action can determine the outcome of the whole, hence the Sage is careful with the beginning. This can be seen in the fields of daily life, government, and military affairs.

63

(MWD 26; GD A8)

Undertake no action, perform no service, taste what is tasteless.
Magnify the small, multiply the few, reply to injury with virtue.
Plan what is difficult while it is yet easy;
Undertake what is great while it is yet small.

Tasks that are difficult in the world [are sure to] begin from
  what is easy;
Tasks that are great in the world [are sure to] begin from what is
  small.

For this reason,
The Sage never undertakes what is great, therefore he can
  accomplish great things.*
One who promises lightly is sure to be little trustworthy;
Treating many things as easy is sure to lead to many difficulties.

For this reason,
The Sage treats things as difficult, therefore he never has any
  difficulties.

Like many passages of the *Daodejing*, this one allows for a variety of interpretations, but foremost among them is a military reading: the enemy who will bring chaos should be nipped in the bud. The *Huainanzi* develops this thought to advocate humanitarian intervention.

64
(MWD 27; GD A6, A14, C5)

While it is at rest, it is easy to master;
While no sign has yet emerged, it is easy to plan.
While yet small, it is easy to nip off;
While yet minute, it is easy to destroy.

Undertake before it has come to be;
Regulate before it is yet disordered.

A tree you can hug sprouts from a downy shoot;
A nine-layered altar rises from a basketful of earth;
An ascent of 100 paces* begins beneath your foot.

Those who overdo anything destroy it,
Those who grasp anything lose it.

For this reason,
The Sage
Is without action, therefore he never spoils anything.
Without grasping, therefore he never loses anything.

{When the people undertake things, always on the point of
    completion they spoil them.}

Therefore it is said:*
The key to approaching things is:*
Be as careful of the end as of the start, then there will be
    nothing spoilt.

For this reason,
The Sage desires to not desire and does not appreciate goods
    hard to obtain;
Learns what others fail to learn;*
Walks* on paths where all others went too far.

For this reason,
Follow* the naturalness of the myriad things and do not dare
    to act* outside it.

The kind of knowledge that is proscribed here is the knowledge of trickery and deceit, which makes people ungovernable.

65

(MWD 28)

Of old, those who fared* by the Way
Did not use her to enlighten the people, rather to fool them.

Difficulty in governing people comes from their knowing too
　much.

Therefore,
To know* the state by knowing is to take a knife to the state.
To know the state by not-knowing is to give life to the state.

(Be ever aware that)* these two are both models.
Being ever aware of the models is called 'abstruse life force'.
Abstruse life force is deep, far-reaching,
And when things reverse only then does it flow with the current.

The image of the sea being lower than the mountain streams is used to illustrate the Sage's way of governing. The streams all flow into the sea, which is therefore their king; so too all people will gravitate to the Sage.

66

(MWD 29; GD A2)

The river and the sea are the king of the hundred gullies
    because they are good at tumbling down,
Therefore, they are able to be the king of the hundred gullies.

(For this reason,)
The Sage
Stands ahead of the people and so puts his person last,
Stands above the people and so speaks with humility.

Therefore,
Though he stands above the people, yet the people do not extol him;
Though he stands ahead of the people, yet the people are not
    jealous of him.*

For this reason,
The world happily accepts him unconditionally, because he does
    not compete.
Therefore, no one in the world can compete with him.

This chapter follows the previous one in setting out in what way the Sage is behind others and hence able to rule them.

67

(MWD 32)

Everyone says I am great, great yet unlike others.*
Now it is precisely because I am unlike others that I can
    be great.
Were I like others then—oh so long ago!—I would have
    become small.

Now I always have three treasures which I keep and protect:
The first is called 'compassion';
The second is called 'moderation';
The third is called 'not daring to seek promotion'.

Now because of compassion I can be brave;
Because of moderation I can be generous;
Because of not daring to seek promotion, I can be the premier
    of perfect ministers.

If today
I were to lay aside my compassion for the sake of bravery;
I were to lay aside my moderation for the sake of generosity;
I were to lay aside my rear position for the sake of priority;
Then I should surely die.

Now compassion in wartime results in victory and in defence
    results in security.
When heaven wants to establish someone,
It encircles him with compassion.*

The *Art of War* by Sunzi, which dates from around the time when Confucius was 50 (*c*.500 BCE), and the many subsequent military books in Chinese tradition consistently hold that the best method of warfare is to overcome one's opponent without resort to arms.

68

(MWD 33)

A good officer is no warmonger;*
A good warrior is not wrathful.

Those good at overcoming enemies do not fight them;
Those good at deploying men put themselves beneath them.

This is called 'the virtue of not competing'.
This is called 'the power of deploying men'.*
This is called 'matching heaven'.
It is the peak of antiquity.

This chapter is similar in tone to Chapters 30 and 31 on military affairs. Here the final line recalls a famous incident in Chinese history. *Zuo's Commentary on the Spring and Autumn Annals of Lu*, in a story dating from 596 BCE, tells how the Viscount of Chu was advised to erect a huge mound to celebrate his victory in battle, but he declined, pointing out that covering the ground with the bones of the fallen is not a glorious thing to do. His army went home mourning.

69

(MWD 34)

In the deployment of troops there is a saying which runs:
    I dare not be an aggressor, rather shall I be a defender;
    I dare not advance an inch, rather shall I withdraw a foot.

This is called,
    'Marching when there is no road;
    Rolling up one's sleeve when there is no arm;
    Grasping when there is no weapon;
    Collaring when there is no enemy.'

Of disasters none is greater than underestimating your
    opponent;*
Underestimating your opponent is to come near to losing my
    treasures.

Therefore,
When armies are raised and are much alike,* then the one that
    grieves will win.

This chapter sounds like the lament of many a teacher. Wisdom is taught, but no one is interested in learning about it because it is hidden in what is very ordinary.

70
(MWD 35)

My words are most easy to understand and most easy to
    practise.
Yet, among men,* there are none who can understand and none
    who can practise them.

My words descend from an ancestor and my deeds are ruled by
    a prince.*

It is only because they do not know that,
For this reason, they are unable to understand me.
When those who know* are few, then shall I be honoured.

For this reason,
The Sage, though wearing coarse clothes, yet bears a precious
    jade.*

Admitting one's ignorance and being prepared for the worst lead one to be open to learning and prudent in acting.

71
(MWD 36)

To know that one does not know is the best.
To not know that one does not* know is the worst.

[Now only if you understand that this worst is worst will it not
  be worst.]

For this reason,
The Sage avoids the worst by understanding that the worst is
  worst and so it is not the worst.

The Sage cultivates self-knowledge and love and does not make demands of the people. This conduct is in contrast with those who do make demands on the people, and who praise themselves and seek their own aggrandizement.

72

(MWD 37)

When people do not stand in awe of the awesome then great
    terror will soon come to pass.

Do not constrict their dwelling-places; do not restrict their life's
    resources.
Now it is only because you do not restrict them that they are not
    resentful.

For this reason,
The Sage
      knows himself yet does not manifest himself,
      loves himself yet does not appreciate himself.

Therefore,
He rejects the latter and chooses the former.

Again, the Sage takes a back seat and so is able to rule. Rushing out in front
would only lead to his premature death.

73
(MWD 38)

To be brave in temerity leads to getting killed;
To be brave in timidity leads to gaining life.
Of these two: one brings profit, one brings loss.

Regarding what heaven hates, who knows the cause thereof?

[For this reason, the Sage also sees it as difficult.]

The way of heaven is:
  not to fight yet still be good at winning victory;
  not to speak yet still be good at replying;
  not to summon yet still have people spontaneously arrive;
  to be at rest yet still be good at plotting.

Heaven's net is broad, yet its mesh is such that none escape.

The Sage does not need to interfere in what happens, because interference leads to injury. The text uses a contrast based on cutting wood, where the job should be left to the master craftsman and not undertaken by a novice carpenter.

74

(MWD 39)

When the people are always not in awe of death,
   then how could you frighten them with death?
When the people are always in awe of death,
    and I were able to arrest and slay the unorthodox, then,
      who would dare?
When the people are always certainly in awe of death,
   then they always have an executioner.

To deputize for the executioner is to deputize and cut wood for
  the master craftsman.
Now of those who deputize and cut wood for the master craftsman,
   few are they who do not hurt their hands.

Mozi, a younger contemporary of Confucius, was particularly famous for his criticism of the nobles' luxury. In fact, this is a common theme for all Chinese philosophers, as we can see here for the *Daodejing*.

75

(MWD 40)

The people's famine
    comes from too many courtiers living off their food-tax,
    for which reason there is famine.*

The hundred families' being ungovernable*
    comes from their superiors having ulterior motives,
    for which reason they are ungovernable.

The people's looking on death lightly
    comes from their superiors seeking to lead a sumptuous
        life,
    for which reason they look on death lightly.

One who has no use for life is worthier than one who values life.

What is supple is alive; what is stiff is dead. Likewise, an army can only be successful if it is supple and ready to yield.

76
(MWD 41)

Human beings in life are soft and weak, in death are always
    stretched, stiff, and rigid.
The myriad things, grass and plants, in life are soft and pliant,
    in death are withered and dry.

Therefore it is said,
'Stiffness and rigidity are indicators of death;
Softness, weakness, (tiny and small)* are indicators of life.'

For this reason,
When an army is rigid it will not win;
When a tree stands erect it will not last;
What is stiff and large lies below ground;
What is soft and weak, tiny and small, stands above ground.

The image of firing an arrow from a long-bow is used to illustrate how the way of heaven works to bring balance to the world. The archer pulls the string and the bow bends at top and bottom. The string is stretched and then released to power the arrow. The Way and the Sage, who acts by the Way, work in the same fashion, constantly adjusting to the nature of the material and not overstretching anything.

77

(MWD 42)

Is the way of heaven not unlike the stretching of a bow?
You bend down the top,
While pulling up the bottom;
You pull back the slack string,
To release it when taut.

Therefore,
The way of heaven takes from what has too much to provide for
    what does not have enough.
The way of people is, however, not like this: it takes from those
    who do not have enough to offer to those who have too much.

Now who can have too much and use it to offer up to heaven?
Only the Way-farer.

For this reason,
The Sage
        acts but requires no thanks,
        accomplishes his tasks but does not abide in them,
Inasmuch as he dislikes being considered worthier than others.

The image of water, which is weak, overcoming rocks is used as the basis for showing why the Sage-king can accept shame and disgrace, because like water these are in a position of weakness and hence, paradoxically, of strength.

78

(MWD 43)

In the world nothing is softer or weaker than water,
Yet there is also nothing that can outdo her ability to attack the
    hard and firm,
For there is nothing that can substitute for her.

Water overcomes rock; soft overcomes firm.*
No one in the world does not know this and yet none can
    practise it.

Therefore,
The Sage's words say:
To accept shame for the state is said of* the lord of the altars of
    earth and grain;
To accept misfortune for the state is said of the king of all under
    heaven.

Orthodox sayings are seemingly reversed.

Although the Sage has the right to make demands on others, he does not do so.

79

In the reconciliation of great resentment,
Surely some resentment shall remain.
So how may this do good?

For this reason,
The Sage, though holding the right tally,* does not use it to
  enforce on others.

Therefore,
One with virtue is Minister of Contracts;
One lacking virtue Minister of Tithes.

Now,
The way of heaven has no family of her own;
She is, though, always related to every good fellow.

This chapter is well known for its rustic ideal, which has served as a model for several similar pieces of literature. The two most famous are those of Tao Yuanming and Su Shi. Tao Yuanming (372–427 CE) entitled his story *Record of the Peach Orchard*. He tells how a fisherman entered a secret and peaceful village cut off from the outside world. The image is clearly developed from Chapter 80 of the *Daodejing*.

Many centuries later, the great Song poet Su Shi (also called Su Dongpo, 1037–1101) wrote a *Record of the Land of Sleep*, where we learn that: 'Politics are simple and customs uniform, the land flat and broad with no east, west, south, or north, the people at ease and free of sickness.'

Mawangdui places Chapters 80–1 between Chapters 66 and 67.

80

(MWD 30)

Let the state be small and people few;
Let weapons of platoons and brigades* be unused;
Let the people respect death and renounce travel.*

Though there be boats and carriages, yet none do ride therein;
Though there be armour and weapons, yet none do take them out.
Let it be that people go back to the days of knots in ropes and
    use them.

They relish their food,
Embellish their dress.
They cherish their ways,
Establish their home.*

Neighbouring states view each other.
They hear the cries of chicken and dog,
Yet people reach old age without meeting each other.

This chapter gives us a set of proverbs. Proverbs play a much greater role in Chinese culture than in English. One of the Mawangdui manuscripts contains over fifty such proverbs (*Four Canons of the Yellow Emperor: Designations*).

81

(MWD 31)

Trusty speech is not embellished;
Embellished speech is not trusty.

The master of knowledge is not jack of all;
The jack of all does not master knowledge.*

The good fellow does not have much;
The fellow with much is not good.*

The Sage does not store:
Having done all for others, he has yet still more;
Having given all to others, he has yet made more.

Therefore,
The way of heaven profits and does not hurt.
The way of sages* acts and does not compete.

EXPLANATORY NOTES

LIST OF ABBREVIATIONS

Chan   Wing-tsit Chan, *Source Book in Chinese Philosophy* (Princeton: Princeton University Press, 1963), 136–76

Henricks   Robert G. Henricks, *Lao-tzu: Te-Tao Ching: A New Translation Based on the Recently Discovered Ma-wang-tui Texts* (New York: Ballantine Books, 1989)

           Robert G. Henricks, *Lao-tzu's Tao-Te Ching: A Translation of the Startling New Documents Found at Guodian* (New York: Columbia University Press, 2000)

Lau   D. C. Lau, *Tao Te Ching* (Harmondsworth: Penguin Books, 1963)

Liao   Liao Mingchun, *Guodian chujian Laozi jiaoshi* (Beijing: Qinghua University Press, 2003)

Wu Hung   Wu Hung, 'The Art and Architecture of the Warring States Period', in M. Loewe and E. L. Shaughnessy (eds.), *The Cambridge History of Ancient China* (Cambridge: Cambridge University Press, 1999), 651–744

The notes are keyed to chapter numbers in the text.

1 *myriad things*: here the received version reads 'heaven and earth'. In practice the two expressions are similar. Both refer to all that exists.

   Be ever without yearning: Wang Anshi (1021–86) proposed that the punctuation of this line and the next should be placed in such a way that these lines are also talking about what is traditionally translated as non-being and being:

> Ever non-being: yearn to observe her secrets;
> Ever being: yearn to observe her bright shining.

   The Mawangdui versions, however, show that such a reading is impossible. For another translation of the terms non-being and being, see Chapter 2 below.

   what she longs for: the received version could read 'her shining', but as D. C. Lau points out, the Mawangdui version decides the issue against such a reading.

2 *Being and beingless*: in this chapter we meet the contrast between being (Chinese *you*) and the Chinese *wu*, which I have transcribed here as beingless. Conventionally these two terms are translated as 'being' and 'non-being' or 'being' and 'nothing'. Unfortunately the conventional

translation gives rise to misapprehension. In the Chinese context *wu* (beingless) is the plenitude that is so full that it surpasses language because no one term can fully apprehend it. It is like the fullness of the mountain which gives rise to the spring of water (being). For further comparisons one can look to Chapter 11, whilst the classic text on the two terms is in Chapter 40.

yet he does not initiate them: the received version reads: 'The myriad things act, yet he does not stop them.' Lau notes that Gao Heng (b. 1894) interprets this as meaning: 'The myriad things act, yet he does not rule them.'

They generate, yet he does not possess them: this line and the next are also found in Chapters 10, 51, and 77.

Tasks come to fruition, yet he does not dwell on them: a similar line is also found in Chapter 77.

3 *He empties his mind*: this phrase and the following can also be read as referring to the people: 'He empties their minds, fills their bellies.' In fact, both Sage and people should carry out these injunctions. All are called to become one with the original chaos time.

   Ever making it such: the received version reads these lines as: 'Ever making it such that the people have no knowing, no longing, so that the astute dare not act. While you, acting by non-acting, discover there is nothing you cannot govern.'

4 *there is something that does not fill her*: the received version can also be read 'there is nothing that is not filled', but Mawangdui rules out this possibility.

   She files away her sharp points: this and the next three lines are also found in Chapter 56.

   She unravels her weft: moralistic interpretations, such as that of Heshanggong, read the character *fen* (weft) as standing for a homophone meaning 'anger' or 'hatred'.

   She merges with the earth: Lau notes that the poet Lu Ji (or Lu Shiheng; 4th century CE), in his *Ode to Feng Wenpi Sent to Chiqiu*, reads this expression as meaning 'merge with old wheel tracks'. The Chinese word is 'dust', hence Lu Ji saw it as the dust of the wheels.

5 *the bellows and the blow-tube*: the bellows *tuo* is of ox skin, while the *guan* is a hollowed-out bamboo. In the received version the second character is read as *yue* and simply seen as another word for bellows. The Guodian version suggests that originally the Way was being compared both to the bellows and to the bamboo pipe, which is still often used for making a fire.

   they inhale less and less: another possible reading is 'the vacuum is never exhausted', in which case this line and the next both describe the limitless capacity of the bellows. My reading sees a contrast between the inward and outward movements of the bellows.

To talk too much . . . chatter: for these two lines, the Mawangdui version reads: 'Hearing (or learning) too much is very exhausting.'

emptiness: traditionally the character *zhong* is read as the 'mean' or the 'centre', but it seems to make more sense to read it as a homophone which can mean 'empty'.

8 *Giving aims to be like heaven*: the received version reads this line as 'giving aims to be humane'.

9 *To hold and fill . . . full*: some translations read this as referring to the taut-ness of a bow: 'To hold a bow and keep it taut is not equal to relaxing.' Lau explains rather that it refers to a special kind of vessel which overturned when full.

fill: the received version writes *man* 'fill', replacing the original *ying* 'fill', which is found in the Mawangdui versions. This change observes a taboo on using the personal name of Emperor Hui (r. 195–188 BCE). Hence the Mawangdui versions must both be before his time.

storeroom: most versions write *tang* 'shrine', but in the Guodian version it is clearly the storeroom, which was behind the shrine.

10 *giving life to the state*: the received version reads 'governing the state'.

She generates . . . them: these four lines are all found in Chapter 51; whilst the first two also occur in Chapter 2.

abstruse life force: often rendered 'dark virtue'. In English the term 'virtue' is increasingly understood only as an ethical word. In Chinese we must also include the idea of the life force of plants. The same title is found in Chapters 51 and 65.

11 *Possess something . . . useful for you*: 'profit' refers to the surplus whilst 'useful' indicates the basic requirements.

12 *The five colours . . .*: the order of these five injunctions here is that of the received version, but in the Mawangdui manuscripts the second (*five notes*) and third (*five tastes*) are placed in the fourth and fifth places.

The ruling of the Sage: the received version simply reads 'the Sage'.

13 *self-inflicted*: this reading is proposed by Liao.

keep of the world: the translation here follows one meaning of the verb *qu* as 'keep', though it is better known as meaning 'get rid of', but this would not fit the sense.

14 *invisible*: the word *wei* (Mawangdui) means the same as *ji* (received version), which here means 'invisible', though some translations give its literal meaning: 'minute'.

intangible: a more literal reading is 'level and smooth'.

One: not found in the received version.

Welcoming her . . .: these two lines are in inverse order in the Mawangdui version.

the Way of old: the Mawangdui version reads 'the Way of today'.

15   *as when ice drifts apart*: this footnote is often taken as part of the text, but from Guodian we now realize it is simply an explanatory note. In Chinese notes are written in the text and not at the bottom of the page, so they can easily be confused with the original text itself.

Hun like a wooden lump: see N. J. Girardot, *Myth and Meaning in Early Taoism: The Theme of Chaos (hun-tun)* (Berkeley: University of California Press, 1983).

Open like a valley: this line does not fit very well. It is not found in the Guodian version. The received version adds it after '*Hun* like a wooden lump'.

He who can make a woman his master: this line is often read as dealing with things at rest (*an*), but the Guodian manuscript reads *bi*, which refers to the vagina. In fact both characters are very similar in form, and it is understandable that confusion arose. As translated here the lines make more sense: the woman gives birth because she has mastered the man.

Only because he does not overflow . . . incomplete: this last line is not found in the Guodian version. My translation follows Mawangdui. The received version reads: 'Only because he does not overflow can he lie hidden and not newly completed.'

16   *Attaining vacuity is perennial*: the line is translated according to the Guodian version. In fact, even the received version can be read with this meaning, but in practice it would more naturally read: 'The highest vacuity is extreme.'

Keeping to emptiness is everlasting: the line is in parallel with the preceding. Many versions read 'silence' for 'emptiness', which is the result of confusion as to which character to write. They also read 'the centre' for 'everlasting', which is a matter of interpretation.

leap forth: some texts read as 'the myriad things come side by side', but the word *bing*, 'side by side', can also mean 'great', hence I translate the verb as 'leap'. We can imagine the myriad things pouring out in abundance from the womb of the cosmos.

heavenly Way: this is the Guodian reading; all other versions read 'these things'. The meaning is pretty much the same: all things pour out in abundance and also return to their source.

By obscuring himself: many commentators read 'to the end of one's days'.

17   *those below only know of their existence*: Chan notes that some versions read 'not' instead of 'below' in this line. The two graphs are very similar.

19   *Cut off sageliness . . .*: the Guodian version has a different order and wording for parts of this passage:

> Cut off wisdom, get rid of debating, the people are a hundred times better off;
> Cut off knavery, get rid of profiteering, thieves and robbers are no more.

Cut off planning, get rid of scheming, the people return to filial piety and fraternal affection.

an affirmative injunction: the reading of this passage is affected by one character, which can be read as *shu* 'belonging' or as *zhu* 'command'. Here I take the latter possibility. In other words, the poet says that it is not enough to have prohibitions ('cut off' . . .); there is also need for a positive affirmation 'look to the simple'. If it is read as 'belonging', then it means that another element must be added to the above three lines. Henricks supposes, not unreasonably, that the addition should also consist of three sayings and hence accepts one possible punctuation of this chapter, by which the first line of Chapter 20 is included here: 'Cut off study and you will have no worries.' However, Guodian A has Chapter 19 without this line and Guodian B opens Chapter 20 with this line, so it would seem it must belong to Chapter 20.

20 *one climbs a terrace*: from the 6th century BCE onward, rulers began to construct huge artificial terraces with buildings atop. 'A Warring States palace . . . was centred on tall platforms that stressed a powerful three-dimensional image and an immediate visual effect. Among excavated platforms, the one in Houma, the Jin capital, preserves a standard design of this type of structure. A road, 6m wide, led to a rectangular ground in front of a series of ascending terraces. The top level of these terraces, 35m north to south and 45m east to west, originally served as the foundation for a wood-framed pavilion' (Wu Hung, p. 670).

21 *utmost life force*: the Chinese word used here is *kong*. Heshanggong says it means 'great', and in this he has been followed by all commentators. In fact *kong* refers to the top of the skull, the hole (fontanelle) where the baby's skull has not yet come together. Hence it can then refer to holes in general, and because this is the point where the brain is, it also refers to what is great and important.

That seed is most authentic: this section gives rise to metaphysical speculation. Most translations ignore the basic metaphors and hence produce readings such as 'The essence is very real; in it are evidences'. Chan notes that 'the essence is very real' is the foundation of the speculations of *Explanation of the Diagram of the Great Ultimate* by Zhou Dunyi (1017–73 CE).

By this we observe . . . of all things: Mawangdui reads *shun*, 'By this we go along with'. The word 'emergence' (*fu*) refers to the first ceremony or capping of a young man. By extension *fu* refers to the beginning, and it is often translated this way. In modern Chinese it can refer to a father, hence Henricks translates as 'father of the multitude'. However, paternity is not the important point here. Rather what is referred to is the moment when things first emerge in their proper forms.

22 *Only by bending . . . Only by twisting*: these metaphors both apply to wood.

Only by hollowing out . . . Only by being used up: these two metaphors apply to water.

pointer of all under heaven: the pointer is what John Major calls a 'cosmograph'—John S. Major, *Heaven and Earth in Early Han Thought* (Albany, NY: SUNY Press, 1993), 39–43. This was a square plate representing earth, with a circular plate above, which could rotate, representing heaven. The movement of the upper plate indicated the movement of the stars. The Sage is like the pointer of the cosmograph, i.e. the Big Dipper which rotates around the Pole Star (the One). The stars of the Dipper reveal the Pole Star, which, being a Cepheid Variable, actually does periodically increase in brightness as the last line of these five indicates.

The Mawangdui versions read 'shepherd' rather than 'pointer'. This reflects another tradition by which the ruler was the shepherd of his people, best known from the title of the first chapter of the *Guanzi*: 'Shepherding the People.' The *Guanzi* is a compilation of philosophy and statecraft dating from around 250 BCE.

He does not reveal himself . . .: for the opposite consequences of these four lines see Chapter 24.

It is only because he does not compete . . . with him: this line is also found in Chapter 66.

is very true: here I follow Mawangdui. The received version writes this phrase with a double negation: 'This is not an empty saying.'

23 *Heaven and earth*: the Mawangdui version seems to omit this response, though obviously it is presupposed by the next line. In fact the omission amounts only to the lack of a duplication mark after 'heaven and earth', something that could easily arise when a manuscript is being copied.

Therefore . . .: Mawangdui has quite different text for the second half of the chapter. Notice in particular how the subject of the last two lines is the Way herself:

> Therefore, for one who acts:
> The Way-farer becomes one with the Way:
> The grower becomes one with the life force.
> The loser becomes one with the knife force.
> For one who is one with the life force, the Way also obtains him.
> For one who is one with the knife force, the Way also loses him/ cuts him off.

When trustworthiness is lacking . . . trust: this line is also found in Chapter 17. It is not found in the Mawangdui versions.

24 *The puffed up*: the received version reads 'The upstanding'. The Mawangdui version uses a verb 'to blow', which is used of rising smoke or dust from cart-wheels. Here it clearly means 'puffed up with pride'.

The self-revealing . . .: the positive corollary of these statements is found in Chapter 22.

Those who have the Way: both Mawangdui versions read 'Those who have desires'. Henricks believes that here the received version is correct and Mawangdui faulty. This line is also found in Chapter 31, where again the Mawangdui version has 'desires'.

25 *A thing*: Guodian writes 'thing', whilst other texts read 'symbol or image'. But in Chapter 21 we find that the two words really share a common reference.

vast: the word *liao* refers to the vastness of the sky: Heshanggong reads as 'empty', which is also the root meaning of 'vast'.

She turns full circle and is not used up: Guodian lacks this line.

She can be the mother of the world: Mawangdui reads 'mother of heaven and earth'.

I entitle her: as Henricks points out, the name was given at birth and is not normally used; whereas the 'title' was given at a man's capping ceremony and was his public name. Some scholars think the word 'force' should be included here before 'entitle' as in the following line: 'I force myself to name her . . .'

The Way is great . . .: Guodian puts these four statements in the following order: 'Heaven is great, Earth is great, the Way is great, and the King is also great.' The version attributed to Fu Yi (558–*c*.639) uses 'man' instead of the more normal 'king'.

the Way imitates her natural self: some translations read: 'The Way imitates nature', but this suggests that nature is a higher entity than the Way. Others translate the word for nature literally, 'what is so of itself'. I combine both translations so as to avoid the pitfalls of each.

26 *wagon-train*: literally 'light-heavy'.

Only when: Mawangdui A reads 'only when'; all other versions literally read 'even if', but in fact the words used in Chinese are interchangeable in the script of the time.

gate tower: the received version of this line reads: 'Even if there are splendid views, he sees beyond them.' The term 'gate tower' is translated as 'walled hostel' by Henricks. Lau reads it as 'a ring of watchtowers'. Like the terrace mentioned in Chapter 20, the 'gate tower' was developed in the Warring States period as a symbol of power. From here the ruler could observe his kingdom. 'Situated in front of a palace, a multistoried *guan* (gate tower) invited its owner to climb thereon and look out; it thus raised the viewing point, empowering a lord to overlook his kingdom and subjects. But as a concrete symbol of authority, a *guan* was also an object to be looked at, its imposing appearance and intricate design inspiring public awe' (Wu Hung, p. 672).

27 *'Wearing Insight upon Insight'*: the verb used refers to putting one item of clothing on over another. In other words, it suggests a superlative kind of insight.

28 *To know honour . . .*: in the Mawangdui versions this section is the second of the three rather than the last.

   The Sage uses it: the Mawangdui version can be read 'The sage is used'.

30 *After great battles . . . lean years*: this line is not found in the Mawangdui versions. Guodian also lacks this line and several others.

   do not go on to win subjection: both Mawangdui and Guodian agree on this reading. The received version adds an auxiliary verb 'dare', 'dares not to go on and draw strength'.

   he does not boast of it: in the Guodian version this line is placed last in the series of three.

   he does not take pride in it: in the Mawangdui versions this line is placed first of the three.

   When things are mature . . .: these last two lines also appear in Chapter 55. However, the Guodian version does not include them here. Instead it reads: 'Such actions will lead to growth.'

31 *concealing sharp edges*: the reading here is based on the Guodian version. Other versions generally translate as 'let calm restraint be the priority'. In fact the meaning is the same: do not rejoice in the exercise of weapons.

   They should not be indulged in: the received version here reads: 'Even when victorious, he does not paint it in a rosy light.' Mawangdui and Guodian make no reference to victory.

   On festive occasions . . . honour: the received version here reads: 'In good luck the left is the place of honour; in bad luck the right is the place of honour.'

32 *counts*: the Chinese term *hou* refers to the nobles appointed by the Zhou king. Later many of these adopted the title of *wang*, 'king', for themselves. One can translate this name by finding an appropriate rank in, say, British aristocracy, but in the *Daodejing* it is used in a very general sense. I have chosen 'count' rather than 'marquis' or 'earl' because of the original sense of the word. A count is the companion (Latin *comes*) of the ruler.

   Then you must also know them . . . disaster: the received and Mawangdui versions both read: 'Then you must know to stop; knowing how to stop, you will be able to avoid disaster.' It is probable that confusion has arisen over the words 'them' and 'stop'.

   rivers and seas: the received version reads 'rivers and streams'.

33 *To die yet not depart*: Mair makes an issue of this line. He believes the final verb 'depart' is a mistake, and notes that in the Mawangdui version it is replaced by the verb 'to be forgotten', thus giving the reading: 'To die yet not be forgotten is to be long-lived' (Victor H. Mair, *Tao Te Ching: The Classic Book of Integrity and the Way* (New York: Bantam Books, 1990), 118). Henricks also translates as 'to be forgotten', but he notes that the verb could still actually mean 'to die' because the Mawangdui version often uses

non-standard versions of the characters. In other words, the paradox of dying and not dying is intended.

34 *She completes her tasks . . . over them*: this is the Mawangdui reading. The received version makes the myriad things the subject of these two lines: 'The myriad things rely on her, and generate and do not fade away: when her task is done she does not claim credit for it. She clothes and nourishes the myriad things, yet she does not lord it over them.'

35 *Model yourself on*: the Guodian version permits this reading, whereas the received and Mawangdui versions read 'hold fast to' and, indeed, Guodian could also be read thus.

The discourse of the Way: Wang Bi reads, in a less felicitous turn of phrase, 'the Way in coming out of the mouth . . .'.

Yet she cannot be used up: this again is the Guodian reading. The other versions all make this line match the grammar of the preceding lines: 'Using her, she cannot be used up.'

36 *elevate it*: Mawangdui A has a slightly different version of this line, which could be translated: 'If you want to abolish something, you must definitely donate to it.' In the next line the Mawangdui version uses a different verb for 'donate'.

37 *And so there is nothing she does not do*: the received version opens the chapter differently: 'The Way is ever without acting . . .'

act: Guodian reads 'act'; all other versions read 'transform'.

Let them: this is the Guodian reading. All other versions insert 'I', hence: 'I will subdue them . . .'

correct: Guodian reads 'correct'; all other versions read 'subdue'.

what is enough: this is the Guodian reading. Mawangdui A reads 'not to be ashamed'. Other versions read 'have no desires'. The Chinese words for 'enough', 'shame', and 'desire' all rhyme and so could be confused.

To know what is enough . . . comprehend: the reading of this line follows from the above, beginning with 'not being ashamed' (Mawangdui A) or 'Having no desires' (other versions). The next phrase *yi jing* is traditionally read as 'so as to be silent', but according to the early Chinese dictionary, the *Shuowen*, the verb *jing* is to be read as *shen*, meaning 'examine, comprehend'.

The myriad things will fix themselves: Guodian reads 'the myriad things'; Mawangdui B reads 'heaven and earth'; the received version reads 'under heaven'. Also Guodian says that the myriad things 'fix themselves', whereas Mawangdui A says 'correct themselves'.

38 *The lowest life force . . . do so*: this line is added in the received version, but it destroys the pattern of the section.

39 *Lack-Grain*: Heshanggong reads as 'no hub', and explains this as the hub of the chariot wheel.

no chariot: the received version has 'chariot', but many commentaries note that this should read 'praise'. Mawangdui B also reads 'chariot'. Heshanggong has 'chariot', and explains the line as referring to the parts of a chariot. Since the Chinese measured the size of a state by its number of war chariots, it would seem that the reference here is to this practice.

rumble-rumble: the rumble of boulders is the sound of the river, especially in the typhoon season.

41 *hardly*: Mawangdui stresses how it is difficult to fare by the Way even for the best persons. The received version reads 'with effort they can fare by her'.

great mockery: only the Guodian version repeats the 'great' before 'mockery'.

Bright Way . . . rough: the Guodian version has a different order for this proverb: 'Bright Way seems obscure; Smooth Way seems rough; Forward Way seems reversed.'

The Way is great: this is the Mawangdui reading. The received version reads: 'The Way is hidden.'

The Way alone is good . . . things: this is the Mawangdui B reading. The received version reads: 'The Way alone is good at providing and then completing.' The Guodian text begins the line 'The Way alone . . .', but the rest of the slip is damaged.

43 *The softest thing in the world*: this is water.

45 *Great straightness seems bent*: in the Guodian version this line comes after 'Great eloquence seems tongue-tied.'

46 *When the world lacks the Way . . . temple mounds*: in modern Chinese the word *jiao* ('temple mounds') means 'suburbs', and some translators translate it thus here, but Waley argues it keeps its old sense of 'temple mounds', placed outside the city walls. Lau reads as 'horses breed on the borders'.

There is no bigger disaster . . . enough: in Guodian this line appears after 'There is no greater misfortune than wanting to get.'

48 *Should there be something to do*: Chan notes that Heshanggong reads this as a conditional: 'If one likes to undertake activity . . .'.

49 *I win*: the reading 'win' comes from the Fu Yi version. The received version actually reads 'virtue'. Both words are pronounced *de*, and the two characters are used interchangeably.

he merges his mind: Chan notes that Wang Bi reads this as meaning: 'The Sage in the world has no subjective viewpoint.'

The common people . . . on him: this line is lacking in the received version, but found in the Mawangdui and Fu Yi versions.

50 *rhinos*: Chinese archaeology has revealed a number of different kinds of rhinoceroses. By the time of *Homo sapiens* there were Chinese one-horned

rhinos (*Rhinoceros sinensis*) and woolly rhinos. Given the climate, it is probably the former which are meant here. Captures of rhinos are noted in the oracle-bone inscriptions, but generally a maximum of two are caught. In one case thirty-six are recorded, but clearly the animal was nearing extinction. Tigers are, alas, also nearing extinction in China today.

51 *final shape*: Mawangdui reads *qi* 'vessel'; the received version reads *shi* 'outside forces'. In fact both refer to the same thing, namely the final shaping of the material that the Way has generated and life force nourished.

there is none: the received version adds this expansion and hence also adds a 'not' below so that the two negatives cancel each other to produce a positive statement.

bestowal: the received version reads 'command'.

The Way generates them . . .: the received version reads 'the life force nourishes them', and hence changes the subject of the following verbs to the life force. Mawangdui retains the Way as the subject of all these actions. In these three lines we can see the image of a growing tree. The first line refers to the growing seedling. In the second line we can discern what kind of a tree it is, and in the third we see the tree flourishing.

Generates and does not possess . . . over them: these lines are also found in Chapter 10, where they apply to the Sage. The first two also appear in Chapter 2 and the third in Chapter 77.

52 *Bolt your ears; plug your mouth . . .*: this is the Guodian reading. Other versions read: 'Plug your mouth; bolt your ears.' Some interpreters read the first injunction as referring to the 'orifices of the heart' rather than the mouth. The line also appears in Chapter 56.

shall not be well: Wang Bi read this literally as 'you shall not be saved'. From the Guodian version it is clear that the verb used stands in contrast to 'falling ill' in the previous lines, and hence should be translated as such.

53 *mountain paths*: the word used in the Mawangdui version is very rare. It clearly refers to twisting mountain paths. The received version uses a better-known word, generally translated as 'short-cuts'.

54 *uprooted*: the character used in the Guodian version shows two hands pulling up a tree.

protected: the Guodian reading; other versions read 'embraced'. Both Chinese words have a similar sound and sense.

their rituals: Guodian has 'their'; other versions merely imply it.

correct: the Guodian reading; other versions read 'authentic'. Both Chinese words have a similar sound and sense.

55 *adders, and kraits*: the first word refers literally to 'triangular-headed snakes'. Such snakes are the Russell's Viper or Bamboo Snake, which are called 'viper' (lit. bearing live young) in English or 'adder'. In China a

triangular head is associated in popular mentality with poison. In China poisonous snakes, not counting sea snakes, are either cobras (old English asp), kraits, or snakes with triangular heads (various kinds of pit 'viper', though not all are vipers in the strict sense). Here I choose 'adder' for the triangular headed snakes and 'kraits' for the rest.

Fierce beasts . . . grasp him: the Guodian version here is odd. It reads: 'Birds of prey and fierce beasts do not seize him, grasp him.' Mawangdui follows Guodian but drops the first verb 'seize him'.

penis: most versions have *yang* and some interpretations read this as the male infant's penis. In the Mawangdui version the character used clearly refers to the male sexual organ. It should be noted that the Chinese term specifically refers to the sexual organ of an infant.

The epitome of harmony!: Guodian lacks this line and gives quite a different version for what follows. It looks as if the Guodian text is inferior here.

To block life: another possible reading is 'to force life'.

Lacking the Way: literally 'not the Way'. The 'not' here must be understood as a falling away from the life force of the Way.

What is lacking . . . early: not in Guodian.

56 *Plug your mouth . . . ears*: this line is also found in Chapter 52 as part of a longer section on the same theme.

Dim the light . . . dust: this line is also found in Chapter 4, where it applies to the Way.

57 *heaven*: Guodian reads *tian* 'heaven', referring to the ruler. Other versions read *Tian-xia* 'the world' (lit. under-heaven).

revolt: Guodian reads *pan* 'revolt'; other versions read *pin* 'impoverish'.

The words of the Sage say: both here and in Chapter 78 the received version simply reads: 'The Sage says.'

act: Guodian reads 'act'; other versions read 'are transformed'.

correct: literally 'still', but earlier we read this verb in the sense of 'examine'.

I do not interfere . . . themselves: Guodian opens this quotation from the Sage with this line.

I long to be without longing: the received version reads 'I am without longing'. Mawangdui and Guodian agree in the reading 'I long to be without longing'.

58 *people*: here Mawangdui reads 'state', but the meaning is clearly the same as 'people' in the first line.

For this reason: here the received version adds 'the Sage', and hence the following poem must be read as a description of the Sage.

force: in the received version the word translated as 'force' is *si*, which carries a variety of meanings, among which 'straight' is one possible reading.

The Mawangdui text writes *xie*, which means a bamboo holder for the string of a bow. Since bamboo grows straight, this holder would keep a string straight. Hence the image here suggested, that things be left to their natural tendency to grow straight up and not forced into it in a rigid way.

59 *collecting*: Guodian has the verb *bei* 'gather', but all later versions read *fu*, which would have had the same pronunciation in the past. If *bei* is read in its original agricultural sense as 'collecting grain' and *se* in the previous line as 'storing', then we can see that the basic metaphor here is derived from agriculture. Other readings give a moral interpretation. *Se* is then read as 'frugality', whilst *bei/fu* is read as 'submission' (Wang Bi) or 'recovery' (the historian and statesman Sima Guang, 1019–86).

essentials: most versions take this line literally, which produces the reading, 'When you have the mother of the country . . .', and then explain that this mother is the Way. However, the word *mu* 'mother' also means essentials, and the word *zhi* 'of' can stand for *zhi* 'will-power'. Hence it makes more sense to read this as 'apply will-power to the essentials', especially since there is no mention of any 'mother' of the country in the preceding line.

60 *Their life forces intermingle . . . them*: both sages and ghosts share a similar kind of power. But as Chan notes, Hanfei understood this line to mean 'virtue will be accumulated in both for the benefit of the people'.

61 *It is because of her stillness . . . position*: in the received version this passage is very confused.

she shall be taken over: here the Mawangdui version has clarified the grammar.

embrace and feed people: the great state plays a female role, holding her husband and feeding her children.

enter in and serve people: the small state plays a male role, penetrating his wife and serving her children.

62 *reservoir*: no extant version actually has the reading 'reservoir'. The received version reads *ao*, the south-west corner of a house where treasure was kept. Mawangdui reads *zhu*, drainage channel. The problem with the Mawangdui reading is that it could not possibly rhyme with treasure (*bao*) and protector (*bao*) in the next two lines. However, it may indicate that the traditional *ao* was originally a similar word meaning 'reservoir' or 'bay', also read *ao*.

Fawning: in the received version the word translated here as 'fawning' (literally 'honour') is added on to the end of this line, to read 'bargaining for honours'.

bribing: this is the Mawangdui reading, as above, and makes sense of what had been rather incomprehensible in the received version.

Three Ministers: Henricks notes that these were the ministers of education, war, and works. In the Han dynasty their roles fell into disuse and the

Three Dukes—Grand Preceptor, Grand Mentor, and Grand Guardian—
gained in prominence. Hence the received version here reads 'Three
Dukes', according to Han custom.

followed by: this can also be read as 'preceded by'.

this: the received version adds 'this Way'; similarly in the next line.

63 *accomplish great things*: Chapter 34 has a similar line but it refers to the
Sage; here the line refers to what the Sage does.

64 *An ascent of 100 paces*: 160 metres. In Chapter 20 we saw that people would
ascend terraces in the Spring at Chinese New Year. Rulers built tall platforms to intimidate other states and display their own power. One in the
southern state of Chu is said to have been *c*.160 m high; another in the cen-
tral state of Wei was named the Platform Reaching Midway to Heaven (see
Wu Hung, p. 670). In the received version this line has been changed to 'A
journey of 1,000 *li*' (a *li* is a third of a mile).

Therefore it is said: this is the Mawangdui reading. The received version
simply reads 'Therefore'.

The key to approaching things is: this line is only found in the Guodian
version.

Learns what . . . learn: since the verbs 'to learn' and 'to teach' could be
written the same way, in Guodian this line could also read: 'He teaches
what others fail to teach.'

Walks: the verb *fu* literally means to 'walk on', though it is more usually
read as 'return to'.

Follow: in reading the verb here as 'follow' I am following Liao. Most commentators read it as 'help'.

dare to act: Guodian A is even more restricting: 'cannot act outside it'.

65 *fared*: the received version reads 'those who were good at faring'.

To know: the received version here and in the next line reads 'govern'.

Be ever aware that: this injunction is not found in the received
version.

66 *stands ahead . . . jealous of him*: my translation follows the order in Guodian,
where the four lines form a set according to the pattern A, B,
B′, A′. Mawangdui A keeps a similar pattern but in reverse order: B, A, A′,
B′. Mawangdui B and the received version use a different pattern: B, A, B′,
A′. Both Mawangdui versions read the initial half of A and B as
'If the Sage desires to . . .'; in the received version this formulation is used
only for the A clause.

67 *I am great . . . others*: The received version changes the subject from 'I'
to 'my Way'. This affects the whole passage, which would then
read: 'Everyone says my Way is great, seemingly unlike all others. Now it
is precisely because of greatness that she seems to be unlike others. Were
she like others, then, oh, so long ago she would have been small.'

It encircles him with compassion: the received version reads slightly differently: 'When heaven wants to save someone, it defends him with compassion.'

68 *warmonger*: Wang Bi tells us that this means that the officers do not run ahead. Waley suggests that the officers would have been in chariots, and so translates 'charioteers do not rush forward'.

the power of deploying men: this follows the received version and balances the preceding phrase, but the Mawangdui version simply reads 'deploying men'.

69 *underestimating your opponent*: Mawangdui literally reads: 'Of disasters none is greater than (thinking you have no) opponent.'

are much alike: Mawangdui stresses that the armies are equal in all respects except in their attitude to battle. One side is sorry about the need to fight and hence that side will win. I have followed this translation. The received version does not stress equality. It reads: 'When armies attack and fight each other . . .'

70 *among men*: the received version reads 'in the world.'

My words descend . . . prince: Mawangdui B reads: 'My words are ruled by a prince and my deeds descend from an ancestor.'

those who know: here the received version adds 'me'.

precious jade: in Confucius' *Analects*, jade refers to political ability.

71 *To not know that one does not know*: Mawangdui A has this second 'not', but it is omitted in all other versions.

75 *The people's famine . . . famine*: the grammar of these three observations is difficult. In the second it is clearly the case that the first and third parts of each line refers to the people and the second part to the ruler. In the received version this structure is also clear for the third observation. We must suppose the same for the first.

ungovernable: Mawangdui; received version 'difficult to govern'.

76 *tiny and small*: Mawangdui A is the only text with 'tiny and small'.

78 *Water overcomes rock . . . firm*: the received version reads: 'Soft overcomes firm; weak overcomes hard.'

is said of: Mawangdui; received version 'is to be'.

79 *right tally*: only the Mawangdui A text reads 'right'; all other versions read 'left'. The right tally was the important part and could be used to demand payment in case of default.

80 *platoons and brigades*: interpretations of this line vary widely. Some read it as referring to quantities of instruments (not necessarily weapons). Others see it as referring to military divisions (tens and hundreds). The Mawangdui version does not help to resolve this issue.

renounce travel: the verb 'renounce' (*yuan*) was misread as the adjective 'far' (also *yuan*) and a negative added, so the received version reads 'not travel far'.

They cherish their ways . . . home: the received version inverts the order of the last two lines: 'Establish their homes; cherish their ways.'

81 *does not master knowledge*: in the received version this proverb comes third in the series of three.

The fellow with much is not good: the received version reads: 'The good fellow does not argue; the argumentative fellow is not good.'

The way of sages: Mawangdui reads 'The way of people', but clearly it refers to sages, as in the received version.

TABLE OF REFERENCES

References are to chapter numbers.